SHERIFF WILLIAM BRADY

(STANDING) *William Brady;* (SEATED) *Unidentified. Photo taken 1871-72 circa, at the time William Brady served as a member of the Territorial House of Representatives from Lincoln County, New Mexico.*

Photo by E. Andrews & Co., Santa Fe, New Mexico

Courtesy R.G. McCubbin, Farmington, New Mexico

SHERIFF
WILLIAM
BRADY

Tragic Hero
of
The Lincoln County War

Donald R. Lavash

Sunstone Press
Santa Fe, New Mexico

FOR
My mother and father
Joseph and Marie Lavash

First Edition

Printed in the United States of America

Library of Congress Cataloging in Publication Data:

Lavash, Donald R.
    Sheriff William Brady, tragic hero of the
Lincoln County war.

    Bibliography: p. 119
    Includes index.
    1. Brady, William, 1829-1878. 2. Sheriffs--New
Mexico--Lincoln County--Biography. 3. Lincoln
County (N.M.)--Biography. 4. Frontier and pioneer
life--New Mexico--Lincoln County. 5. Lincoln
County (N.M.)--History. I. Title.
F802.L7B735   1986   978.9'64   85-8025
ISBN; 0-86534-064-1

Published in 1986 by SUNSTONE PRESS
            Post Office Box 2321
            Santa Fe, NM 87504-2321 / USA

CONTENTS

PHOTO CREDITS

ABBREVIATIONS

AAG	Assistant Adjutant General
AASF	Archives of the Archdiocese of Santa Fe
AC	Arrott Collection
AGO	Adjutant General's Office
ARL	Albuquerque Research Library
CWLP	Civil War and Later Pensions
FC	Frazer Collection
GO	General Order
HB	House Bill
HU	Highlands University
LR	Letters Received
LS	Letters Sent
McNC	McNitt Collection
MNM	Museum of New Mexico
NA	National Archives
NARC	National Archives Records Center
NMSL	New Mexico State Library
NMSRCA	New Mexico State Records Center and Archives
RCA	Records of the Army Command
RAGO	Records of the Adjutant General's Office
RG	Record Group
RMR	Regiment of Mounted Rifles
RUSAC	Records of the United States Army Commands
RVA	Records of the Veterans Administration
SC	Special Collections
SO	Special Order

FOREWORD

History was not kind to William Brady. He was treated as the pliant tool of the sinister Lawrence G. Murphy, political and economic czar of Lincoln County, New Mexico, in the turbulent middle years of the 1870s. And as sheriff when the Lincoln County War gathered momentum, Brady placed the law in the service of Murphy and his henchmen, Dolan and Riley, in their conflict with the rival forces of Tunstall, McSween, and Chisum. Brady's handling of the trumped-up legal moves against McSween, according to this version, led to the murder of young Tunstall, and thereby to Brady's own murder. This happened on April 1, 1878, when Billy the Kid and other McSween adherents gunned down Brady from ambush on Lincoln's single street. It was an atrocity. But not an entirely inappropriate retribution for the sheriff's subversion of his office to partisan purposes.

Now comes Don Lavash to rescue Brady's reputation and repaint the opposing faction in the darkest hues. No longer is Brady the pawn of Murphy but rather an honest, fearless public servant dedicated to law and order and to bringing civilization to this remote and troubled corner of the Territory. Lavash sees Tunstall and McSween as unscrupulous adventurers intent on displacing Murphy and Dolan as the overlords of Lincoln County. When the conflict intensified, Lavash charges, McSween put up the money to pay for Brady's assasination.

This is heady stuff — radical revisionism, no less. It is sure to provoke debate among the fraternity of Lincoln County War students and Billy the Kid afficionados. But Lavash weaves a plausible plot, one that may well have unfolded in reality. Whether or not he has made his case, readers must judge for themselves. What is not debatable, however, is that this version is entitled to thoughtful consideration, for few authorities command the subject and its sources as well as Lavash.

I know this for a fact. Early in 1984 good fortune brought me to Don Lavash's desk in the New Mexico State Records Center and Archives, where he serves as Historian. I had decided to turn aside from Indians and soldiers, at least for the time being, and explore new historical terrain — the Lincoln County War. I discovered in Don Lavash a storehouse of knowledge about my new subject and a generous readiness to share it. I have profited enormously from his counsel.

A mountain of source material illuminates — and obscures — the fascinating and dramatic story of the Lincoln County War. I do not know whether it will say the same to me that it has to the author. But I do know that his interpretations merit respect and serious scrutiny — for he has scaled the mountain I have only begun to climb.

Robert M. Utley
Santa Fe, 1984

PREFACE

This book is designed to bring into focus one of the main characters — William Brady — who participated in the events of Lincoln County, New Mexico during the 1870s. With the exception of carefully selected references based on oral tradition that were recorded in books on Lincoln County, the history of William Brady's life largely has been ignored. Consequently, rhetoric and well-chosen expletives have been substituted for much of the factual documentation.

From the beginning, it has been my intention to evaluate Brady's life objectively. Therefore, most of the accepted traditions concerning him by necessity have been reevaluated or discarded.

Because of the paucity of material, there are painful gaps in the life story of William Brady. Therefore, various aspects of his life are based on historical events and circumstances in which he was personally involved. His military service record has not disclosed any home correspondence that would have provided information on Brady's early experiences in the United States. Many of the essential documents such as notes and letters that most certainly conveyed Brady's view of Lincoln were destroyed by fire. Perhaps in time, some of the materials to fill the gaps will appear.

Shortly after the Civil War, the western section of Lincoln County had been settled under the protection of Fort Stanton. Besides its value as a defense and protection, Fort Stanton supported the section economically. The farmers in the valleys found there a ready market for their crops. Later as the demands of the fort and the Mescalero Indian Reservation increased, cattle and horse ranching became a prosperous enterprise.

Because of its location, the eastern section that comprised the Pecos Valley encouraged the open range and developed under a different set of circumstances. By the time Lincoln achieved county status in 1869, much of the area had been settled by cattlemen from Missouri and Texas. With them came John S. Chisum who with his brother, Pitzer, established their ranch holdings for a hundred miles up and down the Pecos River. The old Goodnight-Loving Trail that followed the Pecos River northward offered the best route for cattle drives to Colorado and opened new trails to Wyoming. Thus the eastern portion became dedicated to American influences, both socially and economically. The western section remained predominantly native New Mexican.

By 1869, the County of Lincoln contained mostly government land and covered almost the entire southeast quarter of New Mexico. Just before the Civil War and shortly after it, settlers of Mexican descent had drifted into the fertile valleys of the Rio Bonito, the Rio Hondo and the Rio Ruidoso. Settlements were established along these rivers large enough to assume the status of communities. The residents of one such community called La Placita del Rio Bonito changed the name to Lincoln and designated it as the seat of government for the new county.

Among those who settled in the western section of the county after the Civil War were the Irish. Most of them had served in the military and were stationed at Fort Stanton located six miles west of town. After their discharge from the army, some of the Irish population eventually settled in the town of Lincoln and became part of the Mexican community.

In its formative stages, Lincoln emerged as a frontier town far removed from more settled sections of the Territory, where law and order mainly depended on what the residents made it. Thus, enforcing the law became a very difficult task indeed.

When curious individuals of a later generation looked back on the 1870's, it seemed to them that the so-called Lincoln County War enshrined forever the horrors of land frauds, outlaws, crooked politicians, swindlers and dishonest local elected officials. The community itself, for all its suffering and sacrifice, had been remembered on the whole as a time when almost every issue seemed to be motivated, directed and controlled by a "Santa Fe Ring." During this time Lincoln, by contrast, appeared to be undergoing internal changes to accept the responsibility of self-government.

That view contains elements of historical reality, but it misses an essential truth about the troubled conditions in Lincoln County between 1875 and 1879. The struggle over Lincoln divided the county resulting in a continuation of the conflict between England and Ireland that has plagued the Irish for centuries. It became a struggle, as the Irish cause had been, that involved among other things commerce and trade, independence, land, politics and religion. Within this hostile, greedy climate in Lincoln, efforts were being made to advance the principles of good government in spite of the growing tensions in the community.

This effort, provoking resistance as it did, kept the community psychologically divided.

I would like to express my thanks and appreciation to many people and institutions whose generous assistance has contributed significantly to this book. I am deeply grateful to Robert N. Mullin, editor of Maurice Fulton's book Lincoln County War, who furnished specific documents on the character of William Brady. Until his death he was generous with helpful advice and encouragement.

Special thanks go to Father Edward G. O'Byrne, Chaplain, St. Vincent Hospital, Santa Fe, who, after investigating the archival records in Ireland, provided important information on the Brady family; Father Patrick J. McManus, pastor of the Cathedral of St. Patrick and Felim Parish of Urney and Annagelliffe Cavan, Cavan County, Ireland for locating the baptismal record of William Brady; Herman Weisner, researcher and historian, furnished essential documents on Lincoln County; Stanley Hordes, State Historian, who read and criticized the work and for his translation of the 1871-72 Journal, Territorial House of Representatives; Richard Salazar, Deputy Administrator, New Mexico State Records Center and Archives for his assistance in translating various Spanish documents; Harwood Hinton, Editor of Arizona and the West, who provided editorial assistance and constructive help on the book; Phil Rasch, noted historian on Lincoln County, for his comments and suggestions; Felipe R. Mirabal, genealogist, for his research assistance; Lynda Sanchez, President of the Lincoln County Historical Society; and Nora Henn of Lincoln, New Mexico. My thanks to Carmen Miller for typing the manuscript.

Recognition is also due to various agencies which supplied vital information. The staff of the National Archives in Washington and in Fort Worth deserves special commendation; Robert B. Matchette, Archivist, Old Army and Navy Branch, for his assistance in obtaining the military records concerning William Brady. I also wish to thank the staff of the New Mexico Records Center and Archives; Special Collections, Zimmerman Library, University of New Mexico; Special Collections Library, New Mexico State University; Rogers Library, Highlands University; Special Collections Library, University of Arizona; Lincoln Museum; New Mexico State Library; Museum of New Mexico; Indiana Historical Society; Oklahoma Historical Society; Nita Stewart Haley Memorial Library, Midland, Texas; National Library, Dublin; Genealogical Office, Dublin Castle; Public Records Office, Dublin; Oifig An-Ard Chlaraithocora Custom House, Dublin; El Paso Public Library; Bureau of Land Management in Santa Fe and Washington; Chaves County Historical Society; Lincoln County Clerk's Office; Lincoln County Assessor's Office; San Felipe de Neri Church, Albuquerque; and the Masonic Lodge, Santa Fe.

I want to express my gratitude to Arcadio Brady, Bennett Leroy Brady, Billy Brady, Max Brady, Mabel (Brady) Neubauer and Bonnie (Brady) Tully, grandchildren and great grandchildren, who supplied vital information and photographs used in the book. Their contributions provided insights into the troubled community of Lincoln, New Mexico.

My sincere thanks to Jim Martin for assistance in providing information on his grandfather William H. "Billy" Wilson. I am grateful to Al Keown of Keown and Associates for the cooperation and information given on William Brady.

Thanks and appreciation are due to all who have had a part in the progress of this work.

To my wife, Bobbie Ann, I want to express my love and affection for her patience and understanding during the years of research and writing this book. Without her encouragement and moral support, the task might have been abandoned.

Donald R. Lavash
Santa Fe, 1984

CHAPTER 1
IRISH BEGINNINGS

Ireland has been in conflict from the days of the Norman Conquest.[1] Subsequent governmental authorities brought sweeping changes and paved the way for eventual English control of that country. To manage Ireland, the English government established the Plantation System, where most of the land originally occupied by the Irish had been transferred to Scottish or English barons loyal to the Crown and England. Various rules and regulations, known collectively as Poynings' Laws, were instituted by the King to compel the Irish to conform to English standards. Later, the Penal Laws were enacted to change every aspect of Irish life including their religion.[2]

By 1829, the quality of life in Ireland seemed destined for improvement. This isolated country had achieved enough importance for the English Parliament to approve the Catholic Emancipation Act. This new departure provided some direction and offered relief to the economically, socially and politically deprived country.[3]

Shortly before the Catholic Emancipation Act had been approved, William Brady's father, John, had become a tenant farmer, built his own home in Cavan Community, Cavan County, and married Catherine Darby on November 8, 1828. Into this environment William Brady was born and baptized according to the rites of the Roman Catholic Church on August 16, 1829. He was the eldest of eight children born to John and Catherine Brady: the children, in order of their birth were, William, Phillip, Mary, Patrick, Catherine, John, Ellen and Peter.[4]

The County of Cavan is in north central Ireland and became one of the original counties of the early English Plantation System. Almost completely surrounded by strong Catholic influence, the county had constantly been involved with the turmoil mentioned earlier. Furthermore, Ireland being a predominately Catholic country, the introduction of Protestant landlords helped to further support the peasant position to find a solution that would elevate them from peonage status. Moreover, the Irish peasant in Cavan and elsewhere would for the next several decades participate in various organizations resisting British domination.[5]

Like most Irish Catholics, the Bradys rented land from an unsympathetic landlord. They lived in the rural community just north of the town of Cavan in the large Catholic parish of Urney and Annagelliffe. John Brady raised mostly potatoes on seven acres of land. He was also subject to a tithe for the support of his landlord and the church.[6]

The features of the Brady home were typical of Irish peasant farmers. Since building materials were easily obtained from the nearby forest, most of the cottages were timber-lined houses and thatched with some stone work to provide for a strong foundation. Usually a stone wall had been erected to designate the property rented by the farmer. Most of the houses contained no more than two or three rooms, the largest being the kitchen area. As the family grew in number, additional rooms were built to accommodate the increase. In most cases, each tenant had one milk cow and some pigs, and usually a horse and wagon and handmade farm tools.

After the Catholic Emancipation, Irish peasants were allowed to purchase land if they could meet the price set by the landlord. Many could not afford the high prices and were forced to continue as they had in the past. However, John Brady purchased some property and later extended his family holdings to more than 11 acres. Also, he and his brother-in-law, Robert Darby, became partners in several more acres adjoining the Brady farm. But most of the land cultivated by the Bradys had been rented land and too expensive to purchase.[7]

Irish peasants who were able to purchase property could not always afford the fertile land needed to raise the best crops. Instead they usually had to settle for the rocky areas and the lands near the bogs. This was not true of the Bradys. Through the joint effort of the Bradys and Darbys some of the best land had been secured. Also, it was the duty of William as the oldest son to assist in the decision making and help determine the best land to buy. Cavan, like most Irish counties, had its share of bog areas, rocky plains and sterile soil. And, if it were not for the rivers Erne and Annalee flowing into Lake Oughter near the community of Cavan, the area might very well be barren land.[8]

All family members shared in the responsibility of the home which indicates a strong family relationship and devotion to one another. The Bradys were no exception. Special obligations, however, fell to the eldest son as guardian of the family especially his sisters and brothers under age. He also represented the family in all cases of stress or need being entrusted with the authority to make decisions for the group.

From the farm, William acquired an appreciation and respect for the soil. Under careful tutoring by his father, he gained a sense of uncompromising principles. But from his own observation and thinking came the personal philosophy that was such a prominent characteristic of his later years.

Educational facilities had been established in Cavan County during the Plantation Period. Most of them were privately owned or built by the British government for Protestant children. By 1819, a Board of Commissioners of Education had been established by the government and new schools were built for children regardless of religious affiliations. Parochial schools were constructed near the church for Catholic children. Before Catholic Emancipation, land tithes were used to pay for Protestant as well as Catholic schools. After Emancipation, Catholic tithes only paid for parochial schools. In 1831, a national system of education had been established for all children to attend through the eighth grade.[@]

Records of his military service and political career in later years have provided further evidence that William Brady attended school in Ireland and completed the minimum requirements established by the local school commission in 1844. He then turned his attention to family matters and the farm. It was a difficult time. The early potato crop in Ireland failed that year casting some doubt on the late harvest, but the potato yield on the second crop seemed much better. However, the years subsequent to this early disaster had a devastating effect on the potato, Ireland's principal crop.[10]

The potato blight began in Central Europe and by August 1845, it had contaminated the crops in Ireland. Later, the soil became infected to the extent that seeds rotted in the ground before they had a chance to grow. Although the potato failed on the Continent and brought some hardship to the people it did not weaken other countries as completely as it did Ireland.

The potato famine that began in 1845 lasted for more than three years. But recovery from the disaster continued in Ireland for decades. An article published in the New York Daily Tribune, December 7, 1846, tells about the conditions in Ireland and specific measures proposed by England to provide aid to the country.[11]

After the birth of their last child in 1846, John Brady died leaving William with full responsibility of the home. Even though the political, social, and religious structures of Ireland were beginning to provide some direction, the economic environment was on the verge of collapsing. By 1847, the potato famine had virtually affected every economic sector in Ireland. During this time, thousands died and many more left the country to establish a new life in Canada or the United States. Apparently, William Brady made an effort to see that the remaining members of his family survived the terrible ordeal.[12]

In July 1850, William became involved with the tenant-right struggle. A meeting had been scheduled for that month to review the law governing the landlord and tenant. During the conference several hundred farmers signed a petition requesting parliament to review the tenant problem. Among those who supported the request were William and his mother, the widow Catherine Brady.[13]

Finally, William made the decision to leave Ireland for the United States sometime during the early summer of 1851. His brother, Phillip remained in Ireland and as the next oldest son inherited the responsibilities as head of the household.

CHAPTER 1
NOTES

1. T.W. Moody and F.X. Martin, eds., **The Course of Irish History**, (4 Bridge Street, Cork: The Mercier Press, 9th printing, 1976): **The Anglo Norman Invasion**, by Rev. F.X. Martin, pp. 123-29.
2. Cecil Woodham-Smith, **The Great Hunger**, (New York: Harper and Row, 1962), pp. 27-31. The Penal Code described by Edmund Burke as "a machine as well fitted for the oppression, impoverishment and degradation of a people, and the debasement to them of human nature itself, as ever proceeded from the perverted ingenuity of man."
3. Seumus MacManus, **The Story of the Irish Race**, (Connecticut: The Devin-Adair Company, revised ed., 1979), pp. 362-67. Moody and Martin, eds., **Irish History: The Age of Daniel O'Connell**, by J.H. Whyte, pp. 250-55.
4. Ireland. Genealogical Office, Office of Arms. **Genealogical Report** (1981), p. 1. (Original baptismal record of William Brady is located in the Diocese of Kilmore, Cathedral of St. Patrick & Felim, Parish of Urney and Annagelliffe, Cavan, Cavan County, Ireland.)
5. Garret FitzGerald, **Towards a New Ireland**, (London: Charles Knight and Co., Ltd., 1972), pp. 1-6.
6. **Genealogical Report**, p. 2.
7. **Ibid.**, p. 3.
8. Ireland. National Library. **Topographical Dictionary of Ireland**, by Samuel Lewis. (Dublin: Government Printing Office, 1937), pp. 318-19.

9. Edward Norman, **History of Modern Ireland,** (Maine: University of Maine Press, 1971), p.86

10. Woodham-Smith, **Great Hunger,** p. 38.

11. New York **Daily Tribune,** December 7, 1846.

12. Edward E. Hace, **Letters on Irish Emigration,** (Boston: Phillips, Simpson and Co., 1852; Albuquerque, New Mexico: University Microfilm, E169.1, A48, Reel 23213, p. 60).

    This study had been completed to provide the census from each county in Ireland for 1841, and then to compare it with the more accurate census of 1851. During the ten year period, more than 30 percent of the Irish population either starved to death or left the country. Accurate figures for the years 1845 and 1847 are not available, but it is certain that the major decrease can be attributed to the Great Famine.

    For example, the census in Cavan County on June 7, 1841 showed a figure of 243,158. When the census reports were taken again on March 31, 1851 the population figures showed only 174,303 individuals living in the County of Cavan. Most of the other counties in Ireland revealed similar circumstances, but in some cases the percentage rates were higher to as much as 40 percent.

13. Rev. T.P. Cunningham, D.C.L., "The Cavan Tenant-Right Meeting of 1850," **Breifne** (Dublin), No. 12, (1969): 111-417, pp. 417-37.

CHAPTER 2
MILITARY YEARS

Upon arriving in the United States, William Brady, along with thousands of aliens from Europe, remained in a temporary holding center just outside the city of New York. Some aliens had been forced out of their country for one reason or another while others had taken the necessary steps to seek out sponsors. For those immigrants who had relatives living in America, the transition was simple. For others, two other options were open: they could either join the uncertain labor force, or enlist in the military. Brady selected the latter and joined the United States Army in New York on July 11, 1851 to serve for five years. He was assigned to Company F, First Regiment Mounted Rifles. [1]

At this time, William was 22 years old, five feet eight inches tall, with blue eyes, brown hair, and a fair complexion. He listed his occupation as a farmer from Cavan, Cavan County, Ireland.

In April 1852, Brady's regiment, under the command of Colonel William Wing Loring, had completed its training program and later, the entire unit transferred to Fort McIntosh situated near the town of San Antonio, Texas. The mounted regiment sent to Fort McIntosh, Texas, provided military support to the new stagecoach line and protection to the wagon trains and prospectors on their way to the gold fields in California.

On October 16, 1853, Colonel Loring appointed Brady to corporal and assigned him to a platoon commanding a squad of mounted riflemen. Brady, a devoted soldier, had a keen sense of responsibility and leadership. On many occasions, Corporal Brady and his squad of mounted riflemen were attached to the patrols that provided military protection to wagon trains from Indian attacks. As the attacks became more numerous, the military patrols increased. [2]

In June 1855, the commander of Company F, Captain Andrew Porter, promoted Brady to the rank of sergeant and placed him in charge of a platoon of mounted riflemen. Shortly after this promotion, Company F transferred to Fort Duncan to protect the settlers along the Texas border. The arrival of the mounted regiment at Fort Duncan increased the military support on the Texas-New Mexico frontier. The unit experienced mostly garrison duty protecting the trade with Mexico that crossed at Eagle Pass. During this time Sergeant Brady, now a seasoned veteran, completed his first tour of duty with the United States Army. On June 2, 1856, he re-enlisted for five years and continued as a platoon leader with Company F, Mounted Rifles. Captain Porter expressed his approval concerning Brady's return to the company: "A faithful and excellent soldier and honest and sober man."[3]

Because of Indian problems in the Department of New Mexico, United States troops stationed at Fort Duncan, Texas were moved to different sections of the Territory. By August 1856, specific marching orders were dispatched to Company F, Mounted Rifles for a new assignment at Fort Craig, New Mexico Territory to support the campaign against the Gila Apache. The remainder of the Troops under Colonel Loring marched to Fort Union to reinforce the post.[4]

Shortly after Company F arrived at Fort Craig, President Franklin Pierce appointed Captain Porter to the rank of Brevet Lieutenant Colonel to command the post. Colonel Porter immediately assembled the troops and ordered training exercises to prepare for the spring offensive against the Apache. By May 1857, the Department Commander, Colonel B.L.E. Bonneville, made final preparations for the Gila Expedition. The colonel and his staff planned a campaign to capture the enemy's most important stronghold in the vicinity of the Gila River. Because of the additional troops at Fort Craig, the military operation against the Apache proved successful.[5]

Company F had been one of the units that participated in the early campaigns against the Navajo and in October 1858, the regiment consisting of 400 men assembled for the march to Canyon de Chelly. During the march, the regiment encountered Indians on several occasions inflicting heavy losses to the Navajo. The Navajo retreated into their stronghold. Then, because of severe weather conditions, the expedition commanded by Colonel Dixon Stansbury Miles, returned to Fort Defiance. The mission had caused irreparable damage to the Navajo and by the end of November, they were ready to accept the peace terms offered by the military. Company F then returned to Fort Craig.[6]

Through most of the summer and fall of 1859, Brady was sent on several patrols into the Jornada del Muerto, the San Andres Mountains, and westward to the Black Range. Further patrols were conducted along the Rio Grande which produced little in the way of noticeable hostility by the Apache. Every mission afforded Brady the opportunity to become familiar with the terrain and the environment.[7]

For the next several weeks, since few incidences occurred, it seemed that the Indian problem in the south had subsided. Because of renewed attacks by the Navajo near Fort Defiance and claims of Comanche and Kiowa outbreaks of violence near Fort Union, Colonel Porter and Companies A, F and I, Mounted Rifles, were ordered to Fort Union to support the post in the event of attack by the Comanches.[8]

When the troops arrived, several patrols were sent out along the Canadian River to find the Comanches. Sergeant Brady commanded several expeditions in the vicinity of Fort Union to map the area but no Indian contact was made.[9]

Rumors of a Civil War in the East reached the commanders throughout the Department of New Mexico. As early as January 1861, the possibility of an invasion from Texas seemed imminent. The following month Colonel Porter and his Mounted Rifles were ordered back to Fort Craig as a support unit in the event of war.

Many of the regular army personnel who did not complete their enlistments were being transferred to the East in preparation for war. Since Brady had reenlisted with the regular army in 1856 for five years, he had only 30 days left on his present tour of duty. He had previously requested an appointment as a lieutenant in the regular army to serve with the Union troops in the East. But conditions had changed. The War Department in Washington recognized the need for seasoned troops in New Mexico to become the nucleus of a volunteer force in the event of war with the South. His request for reassignment did not materialize. Also, Brady had no desire to reenlist under his present status. Therefore, on March 2, 1861, Sergeant William Brady received an honorable discharge from the United States Army at Fort Craig, New Mexico. In the event of war, Brady intended to join the New Mexico Volunteers.

Colonel Porter made some remarks on Brady's discharge concerning his character: "Excellent; a brave man an honest and gallant soldier. He has enjoyed this character during two enlistments in my company."[10]

William Brady was now a civilian living in Albuquerque, New Mexico anticipating that he would soon be reassigned to the East as a commissioned officer with the regular army. But in August 1861, it became apparent that his request for transfer to the regular army must have been ignored. Since he still desired to return to military service and because of the expected invasion from Texas, Brady made the decision to join the volunteer army of New Mexico. He was mustered into service at Albuquerque as First Lieutenant and Adjutant on August 19, 1861, and assigned to the Second New Mexico Volunteer Infantry commanded by Colonel Miguel Pino.[11]

Later, Brady received a formal commission as lieutenant from Governor Henry Connelly under General Orders from the War Department. Then after three weeks of recruitment, the unit left Albuquerque to support Fort Craig in the event of an attack by the Confederates.[12]

Because of the urgent need to enlist additional troops for the defense of New Mexico, Brady received orders to return to Albuquerque. It was his responsibility to assist with the recruitment of two volunteer companies to be commanded by Lieutenant Colonel Christopher Carson and Colonel Ceran St. Vrain to reinforce Fort Craig. As an added protection, the new department commander, General E.R.S. Canby, requested assistance from Colorado. Governor William Gilpin promised help and organized an army of volunteers. Then in February, news of the Union defeat at Valverde, New Mexico, caused the military units at Albuquerque and Santa Fe to retreat to Fort Union.

The final outcome of the Civil War in the Southwest became evident at Glorieta Pass and Apache Canyon. The volunteers from Colorado, together with troops from the New Mexico Volunteers, defeated the Confederates and later, General H.H. Sibley and his command retreated to Texas. Lieutenant Brady returned to Albuquerque and assisted in the reestablishment of the post.

On May 10, 1862, the New Mexico Volunteers were reorganized into the First Regiment, New Mexico Cavalry commanded by Lieutenant Colonel Carson. Brady remained with the new organization and retained his commission. He also maintained his status as Adjutant of Company I, in the new regiment. In August, Carson designated Brady as recruiting officer at Polvadera, New Mexico.[13]

When the last of the Confederate troops left New Mexico, General Canby was relieved as commander of the Department. Brigadier General James H. Carleton and his troops from California had arrived in the territory to support the Union forces and to prevent any further action by the Confederates from Texas. He was directed to take command of the Department of New Mexico.[14]

Early in October, the recruiting service at Polvadera experienced a temporary interruption when a private in Captain Edward H. Bergmann's company was murdered. Since the crime involved military personnel, the Department Commander directed Captain E.H. Bergmann, Captain Jose D. Sena and Lieutenant William Brady, as members of a board of investigation, to carefully examine the circumstances surrounding the death of Private Juan Jaramillo, Company

I, 1st New Mexico Cavalry.

After the board concluded its investigation and preliminary hearing, they sent their report to Department Headquarters in Santa Fe for review. When the review had been completed arrangements were made to send the final report to Tomas C. Gutierrez, District Attorney, Third Judicial District. The district court in Albuquerque issued a warrant for the arrest of a ranch foreman named Harvey Twaddell who had been placed in the military jail at Polvadera. Later, Twaddell was indicted for the murder of Private Jaramillo and brought to trial before Judge Sydney A. Hubbell. During the trial, the jury found him guilty and later, Harvey Twaddell paid the maximum sentence for his crime. [15]

While Brady had been stationed in the Albuquerque area, he met Maria Bonifacia Chaves, a widow. They liked each other and were engaged to be married. But the marriage would have to wait until Brady completed his assignment at Polvadera.

Maria Bonifacia Chaves was born in Corrales, New Mexico on May 17, 1838, and baptized in the San Felipe de Neri Church in Albuquerque. She was the third child born to Jabiel and Yldefonsa Chaves. The other four children were Fernando Rey, Estanislado, Jesus and Maria. [16]

In 1854, Maria had married Juan Montoya, a teamster, who worked for the military. Before the Confederates invaded New Mexico, Montoya had been transporting military equipment in the western sector of the territory. On one occasion, Montoya did not return to his home. The military determined that he had been killed by the Indians while delivering supplies to one of the forts. They had one child named Bruno, born in 1855. He had been with his father when the apparent tragedy occurred. [17]

By November 1862, Brady had completed his recruiting assignment at Polvadera. In the meantime, his future duty station had not been determined. Instead, the military granted Brady an extended leave of absence to visit his future wife in Corrales, New Mexico. There they married on November 16, 1862. [18]

In February 1863, Brady received orders to act as temporary commander of Company G, 1st New Mexico Cavalry assigned to Fort Stanton in the Mescalero Apache country. The fort had been partially destroyed when the Confederates first invaded New Mexico in 1861. Company G became the construction unit to rebuild the post, maintain it and furnish military protection to the local communities. The fort also became the holding station for Apaches before they were sent to the Bosque Redondo Reservation near Fort Sumner in northern New Mexico. [19]

Company G spent most of the summer rebuilding the fort and by

August final inspection of the facility had been completed. Later, fresh troops arrived to form Company A, 1st New Mexico Cavalry. Governor Connelly appointed Brady to Captain and assigned him as permanent commander of the new company. Shortly after he accepted his new command, Brady received word from Corrales that his wife had given birth to William Jr. But military orders from his Commander-in-Chief forced Brady to remain at Fort Stanton.[20]

For the next few weeks, training programs became the foremost activity at the fort with scouting missions a part of the duty outlined by the commander. While on one of these missions, Brady visited the town of Rio Bonito (Lincoln) and vicinity. The beauty of the lush, productive valley that is hidden from view by the Capitan Mountains on the north, and the rolling hillsides covered with forest on the south impressed the young officer. No doubt Brady saw the similarity between the agricultural areas he knew in Cavan, Ireland and the fertile lands below the fort with thinly scattered ranches visible in either direction. He made special note of the area and indicated the most promising farm land. But occupying the land in Rio Bonito would have to wait until he completed his enlistment in the cavalry.[21]

During the following months, it became necessary to increase the number of patrols and scouting missions from Fort Stanton. As a result of continuous Indian disturbances, patrol duty extended west to the Rio Grande. While on patrol, Brady made detailed reports and kept impressive accounts of the missions. He identified the terrain and weather variations; recorded the conditions of the men and animals; and noted specific locations along the route. Brady's accounts of the patrols became useful records for the military.[22]

On April 29, 1864, Brady received his appointment as commandant of Fort Stanton. The military strength of the post consisted of one company of cavalry and a detachment of infantry commanded by Lieutenant Edward Walsh. By August, Brady requested emergency sick leave to have surgery performed on his eye at the military hospital in Santa Fe. He had sustained an injury to his eye while on scouting patrol. After surgery and short confinement, Brady made arrangements to have his family moved to Fort Stanton.[23]

Shortly after he returned to Fort Stanton, Brady prepared an inventory list of supplies for the post. He sent the requisition to the Quartermaster Department in Santa Fe. When several weeks passed without a reply, Brady decided that his requisition had been temporarily ignored. Brady had been increasingly irritated by the apparent neglect of the Quartermaster Department to fill requisitions. Therefore, he sent a letter addressed to the Adjutant General expressing his concerns. He also sent a copy of the letter to the Chief Quartermaster, Colonel John C. McFerran, who immediately expressed outrage at Brady's apparent abuse of procedure.[24]

McFerran preferred charges against Brady for disobedience of orders and neglect of duty. In his charges, McFerran stated that the proper type of voucher had not been sent in to pay for the clothing. The explanations for the need of the supplies were unclear. He further charged that Brady had sent in papers that were not required.[25]

Obviously, Brady's stinging letter to the Adjutant General concerning the overdue supplies for Fort Stanton insulted McFerran. He had been in service for more than 30 years and considered retirement in the near future. The aging colonel prepared a response to Brady's letter and sent it to the Adjutant General. In the letter, McFerran stated he had ordered clothing and other supplies for Fort Stanton several months ago, but he could not account for the apparent delay in the shipment of supplies that were enroute to the post.[26]

A copy of McFerran's letter reached Brady at Fort Stanton. The commandant immediately compiled inventory data, prepared copies of the requisition for supplies and secured the appropriate signatures to verify his actions. Then he sent the entire folder to Adjutant General Headquarters in Santa Fe. If a trial became necessary Brady intended to have proof that he followed the proper requisition procedures.[27]

During the Brady-McFerran disagreement over requistion procedures, a court-martial hearing had been scheduled for December 1864 at Fort Sumner, New Mexico. Brady and several other post commanders were ordered to appear to give testimony in the case. Captain G. D. Morton and the Indian Agent, Lorenzo Labadie, were charged with diverting beef, food and clothing supplies from various military posts in the department for personal gain. From the evidence presented at the hearing, both Labadie and Morton were indicted for misappropriating government supplies. The military could not prosecute Labadie, but a trial was set for Morton the following year. Also, the evidence presented at the hearing convinced the jury that the post commanders were not involved with the scandal perpetrated by Labadie and Morton. After the hearing, the forts were properly furnished with the necessary supplies when the post commanders requested them. Colonel McFerran reconsidered his action against Brady and the charges were dismissed.[28]

After the court-martial hearing, Brady returned to Fort Stanton with special orders to limit military engagements from the post, train new recruits and prepare for combat with the Navajo and Apache. General

Carleton and his staff had been planning the military strategy for the final war with the Indians. A six month training schedule had been devised by headquarters to prepare the troops to take the field.[29]

However, on June 3, 1865, the military strategy had to be altered when two Navajo war chiefs, Ganado Blanco and Juanico, with several hundred warriors, left the Bosque Redondo Reservation. Patrols were dispatched immediately to locate the Navajo before things got out of hand. After Brady's promotion to Brevet Major, the Department Commander, General Carleton, ordered him to take command of the southern forces and intercept the Navajo who were moving in the direction of Fort Stanton.[30]

Early in the morning of June 21, 1865 Brady, with 80 men from Company A and 14 local citizens, left Fort Stanton in pursuit of the Navajo. Within a few days, Lieutenant Walsh and his patrol joined the column. However, the Indians moved quickly, wreaking bloody havoc among the settlements along the Rio Grande. Sheep and cattle were stolen along with other supplies including guns and ammunition. Because of this apparent success, a small band of Mescalero Apache joined forces with the Navajo increasing their strength to more than 200 warriors.[31]

After several days of relentless pursuit, an advanced scouting party located the Navajo stronghold in the San Andres Mountains. It was obvious to Brady that this fortification must be subdued if his cavalry were to charge the Indian camp.[32]

On July 1, the column reached the San Andres stronghold. Brady deployed his troops in a position to strike at the enemy flanks. From his vantage ground, Brady and his cavalry prepared to charge the Indians. Before the order to attack had been given, an Apache rear guard discovered the troops that were concealed in a ravine in preparation for the assault. The Apache was killed, but the Navajo were aware of the advancing troops.[33]

Instantly the Indians prepared for combat. At the same time, the infantry began their attack from both sides. Brady formed his troop of cavalry and charged the Indians, driving them from their position. The Navajo and Apache retreated in different directions making their capture impossible. Both sides suffered heavy casualties.[34]

During the most difficult mission, Brevet Major Brady and his command marched 463 miles in 20 days; engaged the Indians and captured most of their supplies; eliminated Ganado Blanco and Juanico as leaders of the Navajo and halted the advance of the Indians in south central New Mexico.[35]

On October 13, Major Emil Fritz arrived at Fort Stanton and assumed command of the post. Major Brady became the post commander of Fort Selden. He and his command were engaged in several missions to restrict the movement of the Apaches and keep them within the vicinity of Fort Stanton.[36]

In May 1866, Brady transferred to Fort Sumner for the remainder of his military service. During this time, Brady received word that four companies of cavalry were to be retained in service for an extended period of time. He requested Department Headquarters to consider him for reassignment in the new regiment until spring. Since army regulations prohibited an extension on a prior enlistment, they denied Brady's request. On October 8, 1866, Brevet Major William Brady was honorably discharged from the service of the United States.[37]

Brady's military life prepared him for the rough give and take of a raw frontier. After his discharge, he adopted the responsibilities of civilian life with the same composure and determination for success that was evident when he joined the army. His immediate concerns were to buy property, build a home and provide for his family. But, as Brady said later, "this was not a very good time to commence business in civil life."[38]

CHAPTER 2
NOTES

1. Record of Enlistments; NA, RG 94, Vol. 49, p. 15, No. 193.
2. Official Records of Fort Duncan, Texas; NARC, Region 7, M-617, Roll No. 335. AGO, **Enlistment Record,** 201 file, NARC.
3. Records of U.S.A. Commands, Army Posts 1849-1863; NARC, Region 7, RG 393. AGO, **Enlistments 1780-1917;** NA, RG 94, Vol. 52. p. 12, No. 198.
4. Nichols to Kendrick, July 26, 1856; NA, RAC, RG 98, NcNC, NMSRCA, p. 14. [Note: Ref. To NA, RUSAC 1821-1920, RG 393.] Muster Roll, Company F, RMR, August 1851 to March 1861; NA, RG 94, Microfilm, M-1, August 1856, NMSRCA.
5. Garland to Thomas, June 30, 1857; NA, RAC, RG 98, McNC, NMSRCA, p. 15. [Note: Ref. To NA, RUSAC 1821-1920, RG 393.]
6. Brooks to Garland, July 14, 1858; NA, RAC, RG 98, McNC, NMSRCA, pp. 13-4. Bonneville to Lt. Col. Lorenzo Thomas, AAG, October 19, 1858; NA, RAC, RG 393, McNC, NMSRCA, p. 55. Miles to Wilkins, October 23, 1858; NA, RAC, RG 98, McNC, NMSRCA, pp. 56-7. [Note: Ref. to NA, RUSAC 1821-1920, RG 393.]

7. Muster Roll, April 1859; Company F, RMR, August 1851 to March 1861; NA, RG 94, Microfilm, M-1, NMSRCA. GO #11; NA, RG 94, RAGO, January 5, 1860, p. 10, Sec. 20.

8. Stapleton to Porter, January 10, 1860; NA, RAC, RG 98, McNC, NMSRCA, p. 4. [Note: Ref. to NA, RUSAC 1821-1920, RG 393.]

9. NA, RG 98, Dept. of NM, LR, Vol. 10, [no number], AC, HU. [Note: Ref. to NA, RUSAC 1821-1920, RG 393.] NM Census, San Miguel County, July 1860; Microfilm, Roll 713, SC, ARL.

10. Army Discharge, March 2, 1861; NA, RG 15, RVA; CWLP, WO-555-976.

11. Oath of Allegiance, August 19, 1861; NA, RVA, RG 15, CWLP, WO-555-976.

12. **Executive Record 1851-1867**, p. 258, NMSRCA. Brady to Thomas AG, October 23, 1861; NA, RVA, RG 15, CWLP, WO-555-976.

13. Brady to Chapin AAAG, May 16, 1862; Bergmann to Everett, June 6, 1862; NA, RVA, RG 15, CWLP, WO-555-976.

14. Company Muster Roll, July and August 1862; NA, RVA, 211, RG 15, CWLP, WO-555-976; SO #57, Los Lunas, September 1, 1862; Carson to Post Commander of Polvadera; NA, RVA, RG 15, CWLP, WO-555-976; SO #82, HQ, Santa Fe, September 10, 1862; Records of the Adjutant General's Office; NA, RG 94.

15. **District Court Records 1862**; Valencia County Criminal Case #212, NMSRCA.

16. AASF, San Felipe de Neri Church, Albuquerque; B-7, 1835-1838, p. 94; **Baptismal Records,** Microfilm, roll 2, p. 788; NMSRCA.

17. NM Census, Bernalillo County, July 1860; FC, NMSRCA, Comp. T-7, roll 1, p. 109.

18. Widow's Declaration for Pension; NA, RVA, RG 15, CWLP, WO-555-976. Bonifacia Brady signed an affidavit on July 11, 1892 attesting to the fact that she married William Brady at Albuquerque on November 16, 1862. After a thorough search of the files in the San Felipe de Neri Church, Albuquerque, no record of marriage was found. Further investigation was conducted in Socorro and vicinity with similar results. Civil and military files were also consulted but no record was available to verify the marriage.

19. Bergmann to AAG Headquarters, Santa Fe, April 15, 1863; Evans to AAG, June 18, 1863; NA, RVA, RG 15, CWLP, WO-555-976.

20. SO #4, October 3, 1863; NA, RVA, RG 15, CWLP, WO-555-976; **Baptismal Book D, 1862-1868,** p. 33; San Felipe de Neri Church, Albuquerque. (Also see p. 100; Teodora Brady born January 2, 1865.)

21. Brady to Haberkorn, January 1, 1864; NA, Dept. of NM., RAC, RG 98, LR; McNC, NMSRCA, pp. 1-3. [Note: Ref. to NA, RUSAC 1821-1920, RG 393.]

22. SO #15, Fort Stanton, April 29, 1864; NA, RVA, RG 15, CWLP, WO-555-976.

23. SO #31, AAGO, August 13, 1864; NA, RVA, RG 15, CWLP, WO-555-976. (Also see report from Major O. M. Bryan, surgeon, who performed the operation on Captain Brady's eye.)

24. Brady to AAG, October 27, 1864; NA, RVA, RG 15, CWLP, WO-555-976.

25. Charges and Specifications, October 27, 1864; NA, RVA, RG 15, CWLP, WO-555-976; 612=M=304=1864.

26. McFerran to AAG, November 4, 1864; NA, RVA, RG 15, CWLP, WO-555-976; 632=B=612=1864.
27. Brady to AAG, December 7, 1864; NA, RVA, RG 15, CWLP, WO-555-976.
28. SO #26, August 24, 1865. (Reports to Col. Herbert M. Enos, Judge Advocate General, Ft. Union, NM., and Carleton to Brig. Gen. Joseph Holt, Judge Advocate General, U.S.A., Washington, D.C., September 30, 1865; NA, RUSAC, 1821-1920, RG 393.)
29. Post Returns, Fort Stanton, December 26, 1864; NA, RVA, RG 15, CWLP, WO-555-976.
30. **Exodus from the Bosque Redondo**, June 3, 1865; NA, RAC, RG 98; McNC, NMSRCA, pp. 1-2. [Note: Ref. to NA, RUSAC 1821-1920, RG. 393.]
31. Post Returns, Fort Stanton, NM., June 22, 1865; NA, RVA, RG 15, CWLP, WO-555-976.
32. AGO, Old Army and Navy Records, Washington, DC; Vol. 4, p. 181.
33. Brady to Cutler, August 11, 1865; B-419-1865; NA, Dept. of NM., RAC, RG 98, McNC, NMSRCA, pp. 111-15. [Note: Ref. to NA, RUSAC 1821-1920, RG 393.]
34. Santa Fe **Weekly Gazette**, July 15, 1865; Library of Congress; Reel #2, February 21, 1863 to December 23, 1865; FC, NMSRCA.
35. Thomasson to McCabe, August 17, 1865; NA, RAC, Dept. of NM., RG 98, McNC, NMSRCA, p. 115. [Note: Ref. to NA, RUSAC 1821-1920, RG 393.]
36. NA, Microcopy #617, Roll 1241; Post Returns 1800-1916; MNM, Roll M-40.
37. Post Returns, November to December 1865; NA, RVA, RG 15, CWLP, WO-555-976. Records of OQG, Ft. Seldon, NM., LS. NA, RG 92, **Post Letter Book 1866-1871**, Microfilm, Roll 1. Also see Brady to Savage, Post Adjutant, June 23, 1866; NA, Dept. of NM., RAC, RG 98, McNC, NMSRCA, p. 77. [Note: Ref. To NA, RUSAC, 1821-1920, RG 393.]
38. Brady to Enos, August 29, 1866; NA, RVA, RG 15, CWLP, WO-555-976.

CHAPTER 3
LINCOLN COUNTY

Shortly after his discharge, Brady returned to the Fort Stanton area and by squatters' rights selected a tract of land in a fertile valley he later named Walnut Grove. The claim, about 1,000 acres, was located four miles east of the town of Lincoln, New Mexico. The Rio Bonito flowing through the land enhanced the beauty of the area. He purchased on credit, horses and cattle, various types of farm implements, seeds, and building materials. He charged all of this to J. Rosenwald Company, and to William H. Moore and William C. Mitchell under the partnership of W. H. Moore & Co., wholesale and retail merchants of Fort Union.

To the Rosenwald Company, Brady owed $388 to be paid by monthly installments. The final account to W. H. Moore & Co. amounted to $8,132.12. According to the terms of the Rosenwald contract, Brady agreed to pay for the merchandise as soon as he was able with the total amount due in April 1868. However, by April, Brady was in default to Rosenwald. And in May the Rosenwald Company filed suit against Brady to recover the full amount of the contract. However, before the suit reached court, Brady made arrangements to sell part of his stock to liquidate the debt. Rosenwald then granted an extension on the contract and by the end of May, Brady met his obligation.[1]

A few months later, toward the end of July 1868, Brady arrived in Santa Fe to purchase supplies and equipment for his farm. This time he had available cash as his share of the profits received from the cattle sale in May. While in the capital city Brady stopped by the office of the **Daily New Mexican** and provided information concerning available land in the vicinity of Rio Bonito. He further suggested that anyone interested in farming or ranching should consider the possibility of securing a homestead in that district.[2]

When Brady returned to Walnut Grove he was faced with another promissory note to W. H. Moore & Co., Fort Union. The note came due in October and once again, Brady found himself unable to pay the balance. The partnership of Moore and Mitchell then sued Brady for the entire amount of the contract. On October 28, 1868, Brady appeared at Socorro County District Court for trial in which the jury returned their verdict for the plaintiffs. The court then gave both parties six months to reach an agreement and settle their differences. Meanwhile, the partnership of Moore and Mitchell had been experiencing severe financial difficulties. They decided to sell the mercantile business at Fort Union to pay off their debts. Before the sale could be completed, however, Moore and Mitchell were responsible for collecting their outstanding accounts.[3]

Even under these adverse circumstances, William Brady had managed to build a home, fence the area, and irrigated and cultivated about 80 acres of rich farm land. He also planted an orchard and a vineyard. Then William and Bonifacia Brady with their two children moved into the new home at Walnut Grove. Besides William Jr. and Teodora, there would be seven more children born to this union: Robert, John, Lawrence, James, Annie, Catherine, and Primitivo who was born in November 1878.[4]

In the fall of 1868, the citizens of Socorro county elected Saturnino Baca to the Territorial House of Representatives. At this time, Thomas B. Catron had been elected to the same body from Dona Ana and Grant Counties. The Baca family had lived in the territory for generations. Catron who arrived in New Mexico from Missouri in 1866 had served in the Confederate Army. He had studied law and decided to try his luck in New Mexico. Soon after his appointment as district attorney for the third judicial district, Catron moved to Mesilla. Two years later, he was elected to a seat in the legislature. In 1869, Governor Robert B. Mitchell nominated Catron as Attorney General for the Territory. He was confirmed by the council and assumed his new responsibilities on February 7, 1869.[5]

The law to provide county organization designated the county boundaries and authorized the election of specific county officials. During the organizational period the name La Placita del Rio Bonito was changed to Lincoln. Voting requirements were emphasized as well as proof of citizenship.[6]

William Brady was not yet a citizen of the United States when Lincoln was granted county status. Since he had not met the elegibility requirements, Brady's name did not appear on the county voting register. Therefore he could not vote nor could he hold an elected office. The 1868 legislature passed a law requiring each male voter to show proof of citizenship before expressing his right of franchise.[7]

The basic requirements for county organization immediately were to elect a Probate Judge and a County Sheriff. On April 19, 1869, the first election for those offices took place in the precinct of Rio Bonito (Lincoln). The judges of the election were Hugh M. Beckwith, August L. Marie and Henry C. Farmer. The citizens elected Richard W. Ewan as their Probate Judge. Lawrence G. Murphy who opposed Ewan received only one vote.[8]

For the office of sheriff, the voters elected Jesus Sandoval y Sena. Three other individuals were also candidates for that position: Mauricio Sanchez, Silas W. McPherson and George W. Peppin.

The following month both Ewan and Sena resigned. On May 12, 1869, the Acting Governor, H. H. Heath, commissioned L. G. Murphy Probate Judge and Mauricio Sanchez as sheriff of Lincoln County. Since many county residents did not have the opportunity to vote, Murphy requested permission from Santa Fe to increase the number of voting precincts. Then he enlisted citizens from each precinct and began a campaign to register the eligible voters in the county in preparation for the next election to be held in September.[9]

While the county officials were busy with plans to strengthen the governmental structure of Lincoln, Brady had been summoned to Socorro County District Court for the final disposition of the debt owed to W. H. Moore & Co. The plaintiffs requested of the court that the County Sheriff, Andres Montoya, be ordered to conduct an auction and sell all of Brady's personal property to recover their loss. They also agreed to accept as full payment for the debt any money received from the auction. In June under the terms of the agreement, Brady liquidated the debt to Moore and Mitchell.[10]

On July 20, 1869, the same day he became a citizen, William Brady applied for a homestead in the Walnut Grove area. The homestead application included his home, barns and adjacent field situated on the north bank of the Rio Bonito. The Santa Fe Land Office approved his application and affidavit declaring citizenship and sent both documents to Washington to be recorded. Brady also paid the necessary $6 registration fee. According to the homestead agreement, Brady must (at the end of five years) show proof of settlement, cultivation and improvement before a patent would be granted to him by the United States government. Then he could purchase the property for $2.50 per acre and receive a patent to the land.[11]

As a citizen, Brady could now be elected to public office. By August 1869, he declared his candidacy for the office of sheriff. Brady's two opponents were Francisco Romero and Colonel Emil Fritz, who was not a citizen. By this time, the county had been enlarged and separated into three voting precincts requiring extensive travel for the different candidates seeking office.

The election held on September 6, 1869 provided for the selection of one congressman, two territorial legislators and six county officials. L. G. Murphy was unopposed for Probate Judge. Similar circumstances prevailed for Florencio Gonzales who had been elected to the Territorial House of Representatives. Since the Territorial Assembly had not scheduled legislative reapportionment for the 1870 session, Lincoln County was not as yet entitled to a seat in the House of Representatives. Therefore, Gonzales did not attend the 1869 legislature. Brady won his election to the office of sheriff by a margin of eight votes: Brady 102 votes to 94 for Francisco Romero. After the election, however, Sheriff Brady hired Romero as his deputy. [12]

Because of the legal powers granted to their respective offices by the Territorial Legislature, Brady and Murphy were vested with broad powers of authority. At this juncture, L. G. Murphy and William Brady became friends and allies. This precocious alliance had been motivated by factors of similitude since both men were born under desperate circumstances in Ireland. As a matter of continuing necessity, economic and political considerations were garnered for protection and survival. [13]

However, before the election it is unlikely that Murphy and Brady were more than passing acquaintances. After they were discharged, Murphy and Emil Fritz spent most of their time operating the Sutlers store at Fort Stanton. Brady was in the midst of court suits, building a home and arranging for his family. During his military career, Brady had the occasion to meet Murphy only once, in August 1861, when Brady joined the New Mexico Volunteers. At that time, Brady returned all of his regular army weapons to Murphy at the quartermaster department in Santa Fe. Furthermore, Brady had never been involved in military campaigns nor stationed with Murphy at Fort Stanton. For that matter, they were never stationed at the same fort at anytime during their military careers. But the election of 1869 changed the destinies of both men. [14]

The election caused immediate housing problems. Finally, temporary county offices were established in a vacant house in the town of Lincoln. But a jail would have to wait until the county could afford one. To accomodate the county, the Commander of Fort Stanton offered the post jail facilities until better arrangements could be made. In June 1870, Jose Cordova and Marcilino Valdavios of Dona Ana County were probably the first two individuals to occupy the Fort Stanton-Lincoln County jail. They were arrested by Sheriff Brady for stealing an ox from James West. [15]

In August, Brady returned to the Land Office in Santa Fe and filed a preemption claim for 160 acres of government land that extended south across the Rio Bonito from his original homestead in Walnut Grove. He also paid the necessary fee of $1.25 per acre. Under oath Brady stated he was a citizen of the United States; the document having been sent to the proper office in Washington when he applied for land under the Homestead Act. Both Emil Fritz and Paul Dowlin verified the statement. From the reports of the Land Office in Santa Fe, it appeared Brady would soon have full title to the property he had requested.[16]

At the September election, Brady once again entered politics. His concern for county representation to the Legislative Assembly encouraged him to enter the race for the House of Representatives. Brady's opponent, Saturnino Baca, lost the election by three votes. The race was meaningless insofar as representation to the Legislative Assembly, but it gave some hope to the citizens of Lincoln County. Even though the county had not been granted a seat in the House of Representatives, the election had been engineered to support the contention that Lincoln was a political entity of the Territory and therefore entitled to equal representation with other counties.[17]

When the New Mexico Assembly adjourned in February 1871, it failed to reapportion each house as prescribed by federal law. The governor then had the legal authority to devise a plan of reapportionment without legislative approval. Governor William Pile took up the task of rearranging the legislature and provided Lincoln County with one seat in the House of Representatives. However, the Republican dominated Assembly regarded the governor's reapportionment plan as an unacceptable administrative act since it did provide additional seats for the Democrats in the legislature. News of party discontent reached President Ulysses S. Grant and by September 1871, the new governor, Marsh Giddings, arrived in Santa Fe to replace William Pile.[18]

By coincidence, the territorial elections were also held in September. In Lincoln, the Democratic Party emerged victorious. Jose M. Gallegos defeated his Republican opponent J. Francisco Chaves for delegate to congress. Gallegos eventually secured enough votes to represent New Mexico in Washington. Again, L. G. Murphy ran unopposed for County Probate Judge. In his bid for the vacant seat in the Territorial House of Representatives, William Brady, a confirmed Democrat, easily defeated his rival, Florencio Gonzales. When the votes were finally tabulated, Brady received 215 votes to 67 for Gonzales. L. G. Gylam was elected to serve as Sheriff of the county. William Brady then became the first elected representative from Lincoln County to serve in the Territorial House of Representatives.[19]

During the fall of 1871, Brady had been chosen foreman of the Grand

Jury. As chairman, he officiated in that capacity until the opening of the legislature. It has been an historical supposition that Brady attempted to persuade the other members to hand down indictments on those who were not Murphy sympathizers. There may be some basis for this deduction but the available evidence does not entirely justify the conclusion. Already Brady exemplified his leadership while serving in the military for sixteen years. And he took pride in his accomplishments and achievements and always demonstrated a willingness to encourage people to reconcile themselves with others as well as the law. Although ambitious, Brady never sacrificed honesty, decency and justice for any reason, nor was he motivated to do so. It seems hardly credible that he would violate his own propriety of behavior. [20]

In December, Brady left for Santa Fe to attend the legislature. Two weeks later a quitclaim deed was initiated to convey all but 320 acres of Brady's original claim to Murphy. According to the agreement, Murphy paid Brady $1,000 for the land.

An immediate examination of the document would cause considerable alarm as to its authenticity. For one thing, the signature of Brady does not appear to be genuine. But the document and signatures were verified by Willi Spiegelberg and Emil Wolf. On July 6, 1872, the Clerk of the Probate Court, Juan Patron, also stated that William's wife, Bonifacia Brady, approved of the transfer of property to Murphy. But she could neither read nor write. And upon further investigation, no evidence was found to shed light on the disposition of this contract. It should be noted, however, that Brady never filed for legal title to the land except the 320 acres under consideration by the Federal Land Office. He did claim the remainder of the property by squatters' rights. The transfer of funds from Murphy to Brady represented a legal transaction. But the transaction involved only the purchase of title to squatters' rights which is not recognized as a legal title by the federal government. [21]

Early in November before the legislature convened in Santa Fe, the Las Cruces **Borderer** provided some insights on the concerns of the people that several laws needed to be changed for territorial recognition. The editorial specified those areas of importance and insisted that "the legislature should adopt such measures as the imperative wants of the people require. They are chosen by the people for this purpose and have accepted the trust. It should be their aim, and we have no doubt it will be, to examine our schools, our tax and license laws, and the regulations for our county administration. Radical changes are needed, and we hope that every member will appreciate the responsibility resting upon him, and bring to the task a sound judgement, matured by reflection and study. The action of the present legislature will either place our Terriotry in a more favorable light with our fellow citizens abroad or fasten upon us still more firmly the stigma of ignorance and inertion [sic]."[22]

Beginning with the Twentieth Legislative Assembly (December 4, 1871 to February 1, 1872), the sessions were biennial rather than annual. Even though several new faces appeared in both chambers, still the Republican Party held control of the legislature. The Democrats, however, gained a few seats especially in the House of Representatives. Both houses then were charged with the responsibility to enact suitable legislation lasting for two years.

Shortly after the legislature convened, Representative Brady introduced a motion to hire an interpreter for the chamber. The house delegates rejected the motion and tabled it indefinitely. Brady then challenged the decision stating: "that the negotiations of this chamber be transacted entirely in the English language, as it is the language of the United States. I petition this as a right, as a citizen of the United States. And if the natives of this territory desire to dispense with an interpreter, they can do so." The majority compromised and passed a law to have each bill translated in both English and Spanish. The house then approved a motion to hire A. P. Sullivan, editor of the Santa Fe **Weekly Post** as public printer. Sullivan had been identified with the House Democrats and not looked upon favorably by the Republican majority.[23]

The next day a commission made up of both houses assembled to meet with the governor and the Secretary of the Territory to name and pay an interpreter. It was agreed to accept the commission's report. Each house then hired its own interpreter. Following the commission's report, each house assigned its members to committees. The Speaker of the House of Representatives assigned Brady to three committees: Chairman of the Military Affairs and the Library committees, and designated him as a member of the Commission on Indian Affairs.[24]

Two of the more important bills introduced at this session of the legislature provided for an educational system throughout the territory. Representative Julian Montoya from Socorro introduced an act as House Bill 14 "To Establish a System of Schools for the Territory of New Mexico and to Maintain Public Schools in each County." Following Montoya's bill, Representative Brady submitted a special resolution designated as House Bill 15 entitled, "An Act for the Better Organization of Public Schools in the Different Counties of the Territory." Both acts were approved and sent to the Education Committee. The educational philosophies of Montoya and Brady were significant to establish a basis for the drafting of House Bill 36 that was eventually approved by both houses and signed by the governor.[25]

In essence, House Bill 36 established the mechanism for a Territorial Board of Education to be appointed by the governor. It permitted the election of county and local school boards granting to them authority to appoint superintendents of education. Unfortunately, the bill failed to include courses to be taught or how board members, superintendents and teachers were to be paid. Furthermore, the legislature did not provide emergency funds to support the program.[26]

The inherent dislike for property taxes and the suspicion on the part of the people that the newcomers were determined to change the ideas and ideals of their children were the major deterrents to school support. Later, the Assembly sponsored appropriate legislation allowing the counties to collect a school tax to be used exclusively for public schools. The new school law was the first major attempt by any territorial legislature to adopt a set of rules and regulations establishing the public school system in New Mexico.

Representative Brady introduced another bill of political importance to redefine the boundaries of Lincoln and Dona Ana counties. Because of the possibility that it might help the Democrats gain additional seats in the legislature, the Republican majority in the House of Representatives defeated the bill. Midway through the session, a bill to allow foreigners to hold property in New Mexico had been reported "out of committee" and immediately rejected. Later, the committee submitted amendments to the bill and returned it to the full house for approval. Foremost among the amendments was one allowing foreigners to inherit land without first becoming citizens. After some debate, both houses passed the bill and later the governor signed it into law. Brady voted against the original act and the amended bill.[27]

On December 30, 1871, a controversial bill, House Bill 33, had been introduced to reassign the Judges of the Supreme Court to District Courts. The aim of the sponsors of the bill was to move Chief Justice Joseph G. Palen from the important First District in Santa Fe to the remote and less vital district of Mesilla. The bill received hasty approval by both Houses and was sent to the governor for his signature. However, Governor Giddings felt that the judge had been unjustly attacked and that money interests had intervened rather than good judgement. Furthermore, several important individuals were under indictment such as A. P. Sullivan, the postmaster and editor or the Santa Fe **Weekly Post** mentioned earlier. Others including Henry Wetter, Secretary of the Territory, were charged with various types of wrongdoing.[28]

Governor Giddings, outraged by the legislative action, vetoed the bill moving Palen to Mesilla. Both Houses of the Assembly sustained the governor's veto. This act so angered the Democrats that they determined to seize control of the legislature. Under a charge of impropriety in the Taos election, the Democrats along with a sufficient number of Republicans had three elected members from that county removed. They were replaced with Democrats, giving that party a majority in the House.[29]

Under pressure the Speaker of the House, Milner Rudolf, called for an adjournment hoping to settle the climate of ill feeling in the chamber. But after the Republicans filed out of the House, the Democrats immediately began to organize their own legislature, electing John R. Johnson as their speaker. The Democrats and Republicans then established separate legislatures and continued with the job of passing laws. Brady, a Democrat, sided with the minority faction which might very well have caused him to lose his seat in the House of Representatives at the next election. Threats of violence kept the newspapers busy and both legislative groups in a state of tension.[30]

Shortly before the legislative adjournment, leaders of the two groups realized the necessity for compromise. By agreement both of the factions were favorable to a new speaker. They elected Gregorio N. Otero to chair the meeting. Still more resentment filled the legislative halls when Secretary Wetter, who had been involved with the reassignment of Judge Palen, refused to pay the House members their per diem allowance. But later, the delegates to the legislature were paid.[31]

Since the legislature had not considered reapportionment, Governor Giddings then made it his repsonsibility to reapportion both Houses. Under the new program, the counties of Lincoln, Dona Ana and Grant were combined into one legislative district. Thus the county of Lincoln lost its opportunity to secure a permanent seat in the House of Representatives.[32]

While Representative William Brady was in Santa Fe, he decided to become a Mason joining the Montezuma Lodge on January 20, 1872. Although a Catholic, Brady found the code of Masonry to be an inspiration to his own sense of decency and justice. On December 7, 1874, he became a Master Mason.[33]

After the legislature adjourned in February, Brady returned to Lincoln and his family. The welcome home party was typical for the Bradys as William usually distributed gifts to every member of his family. For his wife, Brady always brought an article of exceptional quality.

Brady's devotion to his family is best described by Jesus Ortega who resided in Lincoln and was a close friend of the family:

"Many possibly most Southern New Mexico Anglos married women of Spanish (Mexican) extraction, and as a rule treated their wives as servants seldom taking wives along to social gatherings or appearing with them in public. Many were attractive, not to say beautiful, and few wives possessed wardrobes more than work clothes. William Brady was an exception. He escorted Mrs. Brady to and from services at the Catholic chapel, and he never attended social gatherings without his wife on his arm. She never appeared gaudily dressed, but her garments were always in good taste. Brady never returned from Santa Fe without a handsome garment for his wife." [34]

During the next several months, Brady spent most of the time attending to the operation of his farm. Planting time and the early hay season kept him busy and away from town. Around the first of July, word reached Brady from Santa Fe that the Land Office had not received proof of his citizenship. The information surprised and puzzled him because one of the provisions mandated by the Homestead and Preemption Acts was proof of citizenship before clear title to government property is approved. He had complied with the law. On July 20, 1872, exactly three years from the date he first became a citizen, William Brady appeared before the District Court in Lincoln to verify his citizenship. The Court Clerk, Ira M. Bond, signed the certificate of citizenship witnessed by William W. Martin and Juan B. Patron. [35]

However, final consideration granting title to Brady on the 320 acres of land under deliberation by the Land Office in Washington had not been determined. In 1874, and still waiting for his government patents, the Land Office informed Brady that he had to furnish proof of military service to complete the Homestead requirements. After his service records were properly notarized by J. R. Bolton, Brady sent the documents to Santa Fe.

A few weeks later he again received word from the Land Office that his Preemption Certificate would be suspended until he could verify his citizenship. Once more it appeared that his citizenship papers were either lost or misplaced. The frustration he must have felt is impossible to appreciate. Surely he was discouraged, disappointed and disillusioned. But on March 30, 1874, the registrar, Abraham G. Hoyt, sent a letter to the commissioner in Washington at last verifying Brady's citizenship. [36]

To complicate matters, Registrar Hoyt resigned soon after sending the letter to Washington and Joseph D. Seria replaced Hoyt as the new registrar in Santa Fe. About the same time, President Grant appointed S. S. Burdett as the new Land Commissioner in Washington. Under these circumstances, additional information became necessary to authorize

Brady's patents.

On January 13, 1875, the Santa Fe Land Office prepared to move part of its office to Mesilla, New Mexico. While packing up the records the registrar, Joseph D. Seria, uncovered Brady's certificate of citizenship and military service record and immediately sent them to Washington.[37]

In March, William received a patent to 160 acres he requested under the Preemption Act authorized by congress. After more than six years of patience and complying with the law, Brady acquired title to part of his property from the federal government.[38]

However, legal title to an additonal 160 acres under the Homestead Act was still delayed. His military and citizenship status had to be verified by a separate department in Washington. Finally, two months later, his Homestead patent was approved.[39]

When Brady returned from the legislature, he immediately announced his candidacy for the office of Probate Judge. His opponent was Saturnino Baca. In the election held on April 8, 1872, Baca emerged victorious as the undisputed choice of the people. Brady had been one of the judges in Precinct 1. The Clerk of the Court, Juan Patron, noted that Brady did not sign the election results. After certifying the election, Patron enclosed a letter with the transcript to the Secretary of the Territory.

In the letter, Patron explained to the secretary that the poll book of Precinct 1 had been signed by only two of the judges of election. "Mr. Brady, one of the judges of the election, had refused to sign the book without giving any reason for such a conduct."[40]

Perhaps there were several good reasons. Whatever they may have been, certainly Brady had sufficient knowledge about procedure to validate his conduct. Possibly he felt the election failed to adhere to proper standards of conduct and he did not want to be associated with impropriety. He either suspected something was wrong and could not prove it, or he knew what happened and refused to be a party to what he considered a fixed election. To Brady, conscientious work had always been careful and exact. He probably questioned the results of the election and did not receive satisfactory answers. Furthermore, Brady had been a judge of elections in the past and there seems to be no indication that he had ever refused to sign a poll book.

During the same month, Brady had been selected for jury duty and served as foreman. The spring term of court heard several types of cases from murder to civil suits on past due notes. Certain prominent citizens, through the courts, had found a legal method to appropriate land and personal property from those individuals who could not pay their debts. J. B. Wilson, John Chisum, James J. Dolan and many other residents of

41

Lincoln were identified as plaintiffs in civil suits to reclaim debts owed to them. Several merchants in the Lincoln-Fort Stanton area including Juan Patron, Isaac Ellis and Sons and Jose Montano took advantage of the law to recover their losses. Lawrence G. Murphy and Emil A. Fritz owned and maintained the most prosperous mercantile store in town. They became involved in civil suits with the results most favorable to the plaintiffs. [41]

Murphy and Fritz were mustered out of the army at Fort Union in 1866. That year they established the partnership of L. G. Murphy & Co. and opened a store adjacent to Fort Stanton. By 1871, Vincent Colyer, Commissioner Indian Affairs, reported to the Secretary of the Interior that the Mescalero Apache at the fort were under good managment. Through the efforts of A. J. Curtis, Indian Agent, L. G. Murphy and Emil Fritz peace had been maintained. Later, a permanent reservation for the Indians would be selected. [42]

During this time, L. G. Murphy & Co. managed to control much of the business activities in the area. Murphy also controlled most of the wagon trains bringing supplies to the post and producers had to sell to him at his prices. The local farmers and ranchers also wanted more of the profits on goods sold to the military. By 1872, the federal government had surveyed the Fort Stanton area, setting aside thousands of acres of land as a reserve for the Mescalero Apache. Then in June 1873, an executive order established the Mescalero Apache Indian Reservation. [43]

The Sutlers store owned by Murphy & Co. had been included in the government survey. But private citizens were not allowed to own property on government land. On June 13, 1873, a quitclaim deed transferring the property owned by Murphy & Co. to Fort Stanton was completed. L. Edwin Dudley, Superintendent of Indian Affairs for New Mexico, acting for the United States government, then paid Murphy $8,000 for the entire inventory including the Sutlers store. When Dudley returned to Fort Stanton in September 1873, Murphy & Co. had already left the post. [44]

During the course of this event, there were persistant allegations and complaints of monopolizing the business activities at the post by Murphy and Fritz which seemed to have hastened the departure of Murphy & Co. Another incident involved the arrest of Captain James F. Randelett after a complaint of assault had been charged against him by James J. Dolan, a clerk in Murphy's store. It seems that the altercation was the result of some disagreement over a debt owed to Dolan. Randelett posted bail and left the territory for Fort Levenworth, Kansas. He was later identified with the Harrell Brothers and indicted for murder. [45]

Although Murphy and Fritz had expanded their business expertise to land, the mercantile interest was the most important. When the store was sold to the government, Murphy and Fritz moved to Lincoln and began similar operations there. However, Fritz became ill, and in June left for Germany where he died the following year. On April 29, 1873, just three months before he left the country, Emil Fritz became a citizen of the United States. [46]

In the fall and winter of 1873, the condition of affairs in Lincoln were altered drastically, establishing a pattern of indiscriminate violence and murder. Perhaps the most outrageous incident occurred in December of that year. A Texas group called the Harrell Brothers had made a hasty retreat from Lampasas County, Texas to avoid the law. Moving to New Mexico they settled on the Ruidoso and several of the group went to Lincoln to celebrate their achievement. A series of verbal confrontations took place resulting in a shooting in which Constable Juan Martinez was killed, as were Jack Gylam and Ben Harrell. [47]

Several days later, the Harrell clan and other nearby residents entered Lincoln determined to have revenge on those who were responsible for killing their brother and friends. Reports on the violence contained evidence that every man in the mob was armed to the teeth and spoiling for a fight. When the angry group reached town they began shooting up the place, killing several people including Isidro Patron, father of Juan Patron. [48]

As a result of these disturbing conditions, a mass meeting was held on January 9, 1874 to initiate procedures for the protection of the community. For some unknown reason, the Justice of the Peace and the Probate Judge, Jacinto Sanchez, were not available to provide the leadership necessary for the protection of the people. Therefore, L. G. Murphy took charge and presided at the meeting. James Dolan was elected secretary. The concerned membership appointed Jose Montano, L. G. Murphy and William Brady to organize a vigilante committee to preserve the peace and order in Lincoln. Further requests were made to Governor Giddings and General Granger, in command of the federal troops, to provide aid when the emergency arose. However, the Harrells left the county and headed for Texas. [49]

Beyond any doubt, though, the Harrell incident had proved conclusively that the town of Lincoln had furnished little in the way of strong leadership and protection. Even the military was reluctant to provide any support or assistance when it was needed. This episode of destruction and murder was to become familiar in Lincoln County in the days to come.

Meanwhile, conditions returned to normal and most of the farmers and ranchers returned to their homes. However, some left the community to settle in more peaceful surroundings. But Brady's farm at Walnut Grove had suffered considerably. Important work had not been done. During this time Brady managed to hire some additional ranch hands to help brand his cattle. Brady registered his brand as BB on the left hip with ear marks split in both ears.[50]

When Lincoln county organized in 1869, strong leadership prevailed. Laws governing new counties were promulgated by the Territorial Legislature and under this mandate, authority to implement local ordinances had been granted to the Probate Judge. Rules governing the sheriff's office were carefully outlined by the same legally constituted body. In essence, the County Sheriff had been authorized by the legislature to enforce the law. Some individuals such as William Brady had pressed for county recognition in Santa Fe. He was successful in this and represented his county in the Territorial House of Representatives.

By 1873, the leadership in Lincoln had changed. Crime and violence had reached crisis proportions and only minimal restraint was placed on any perpetrators. Many citizens of Lincoln County expressed their concerns and organized a vigilante committee. The community now knew that strong leadership and enforcement of the law was a necessity.

CHAPTER 3
NOTES

1. Socorro County, **District Court Record Book #3** (1865-1873), Civil Case #24, p. 119. NMSRCA
2. **Daily New Mexican,** July 23, 1868. NMSL.
3. Socorro County, **District Court Record Book #3,** (1865-1873), Civil Case #60, p. 146. NMSRCA.
4. NM Census, Lincoln County, June 5, 1880, p. 13. NMSRCA.
5. **Executive Record 1867-1882;** January 16, 1869. p. 25. The Governor approved an act entitled, **Un Acto Judicial creando y organizando el Condado de Lincoln.** NMSRCA.
6. New Mexico Statutes Codification 1915, pp. 400-1. NMSRCA.
7. Robert W. Larson, **New Mexico's Quest for Statehood, 1846-1912,** (Albuquerque: The University of New Mexico Press, 1968), p. 90.

8. Lincoln County, **Poll Book of Election,** April 19, 1869. NMSRCA. (See **Executive Record 1867-1882,** p. 32.) NMSRCA.

9. **Executive Record 1867-1882,** p. 33. NMSRCA.

10. Socorro County, **District Court Record Book** #3 (1865-1873), Civil Case #89, pp. 193-4. NMSRCA.

11. Homestead Application #7, July 20, 1869; NA, RG 49; SFNM File #4. (See **Congressional Record,** 37th Congress 1862, Session 2; **Homestead Act,** Ch. 75, Sec. 2, p. 392.)

12. Lincoln County, **Poll Book of Election,** March 1, 1869. NMSRCA.

13. General Laws of New Mexico 1882; **Probate Courts;** Art. 11, Ch. 22, pp. 81-114: **Sheriff;** Art. 59, ch. 94, pp. 527-36. NMSRCA.

14. Muster Roll, August 1861; 2nd New Mexico Infantry. NA, RG 94.

15. Lincoln County, **Probate Court Record,** [no number], June 3, 1870. NMSRCA.

16. Preemption Rights Affidavit, Cash Entry Certificate, August 6, 1870; NA, RG 49; SFNM File #10. (See **Congressional Record,** 27th Congress 1841, Session 1, **Preemption Rights Act,** Ch. 16. Sec. 10, p. 455.)

17. Lincoln County, **Poll Book of Election,** September 5, 1870. NMSRCA.

18. Larson, **Quest for Statehood,** p. 94.

19. Lincoln County, **Poll Book of Election,** September 4, 1871. NMSRCA.

20. Lincoln County, **District Court Record,** (1871-1872). NMSRCA. (See Department of the Interior, **Appointment Papers,** Territory of New Mexico 1850-1907; Microfilm Roll #12. NMSL, LC, SW, 978.9, 16luI.)

    In May 1873, William Brady's name had been submitted to the Board of Indian Commissioners, Washington, DC, for consideration as Indian Agent for the Mescalero Apache Indians, Fort Stanton, New Mexico. Usually a formal letter is sent by the person seeking the appointment. However, Brady had not applied for the position. Instead, Lawrence G. Murphy and Bishop John B. Lamy recommended Brady to the post. Brady was not selected.

21. Quitclaim Deed from Brady to Murphy; **Deed Book E-Misc.,** pp. 46-8. Clerk's Office, Lincoln County Courthouse, Carrizozo.

22. **The Borderer,** November 22, 1871. EPPL.

23. **House Journal** (1871-1874), p. 4. NMSRCA.

24. Ibid. p. 27.

25. Ibid., p. 28. (See also HB No's. 14 and 15; Legislative Acts (1871-1872). NMSRCA.)

26. Legislative Acts (1871-1872), HB #36, January 1872. NMSRCA.

27. **House Journal** (1871-1874), pp. 39-40. NMSRCA.

28. Larson, **Quest for Statehood,** p. 96.

29. **House Journal** (1871-1874), p. 89. NMSRCA.

30. Larson, **Quest for Statehood,** p. 98. (See **House Journal** (1871-1874), pp. 106-8. NMSRCA.)

31. **Weekly Post,** Santa Fe, NM., February 10, 1872. Microfilm Roll #345. MNM.

32. **Daily New Mexican,** Santa Fe, NM., March 22, 1872. NMSL.

33. Masonic Lodge Record Book, 1872. Montezuma Lodge, Santa Fe. (Letter

from William A. Keleher, Lincoln County Historian, to Robert Mullin, November 1919. Original in Author's Collection courtesy of Robert Mullin, December 10, 1979.

"As a young man William Brady became a volunteer member of the New Mexico Volunteers and later became a member of the New Mexico Cavalry. where a record of valiant service brought him a promotion to Major. When most regular army troops were transferred out of New Mexico, Indian disturbances broke out all over the territory and the New Mexico Volunteers were kept busy and no officer won more praise for restricting the Indians than did Wm. Brady. The great love of his career was as a member of the Masonic Lodge. As sheriff he was under the orders of certain politicians and expressed himself as being uncomfortable in complying with orders which violated his sense of decency and the code of Masonry."

34. Jesus Ortega; interview held by Robert Mullin, Lincoln, June 12, 1913. Original in Author's Collection, courtesy of Robert Mullin, December 10, 1979.
35. Certificate of Naturalization, July 20, 1872; NA, RG 49, Vol. 2. p. 94.
36. Hoyt to Drummond, March 30, 1874; NA, RG 49.
37. Seria to Burdett, January 13, 1875; NA, RG 49.
38. Bureau of Land Management, **Preemption Patent Book,** March 25, 1875, Certificate #10, p. 94. SFNM. (See X-F Patent Book pp. 235-36, Lincoln County Clerk's Office, Carrizozo.)
39. Bureau of Land Management, **Homestead Patent Book,** May 10, 1875, Application #7, Certificate #4, p. 3. SFNM. (See **Xa Patent book,** p. 60, Lincoln County Clerk's Office, Carrizozo.)
40. Lincoln County Records, **Certificate of Election 1872.** NMSRCA.
41. Lincoln County, **District Court Records** (1873-1879). NMSRCA.
42. Report of the Secretary of the Interior to the 42nd Congress, session 2, 1871. **Executive Document 1,** Part 5, serial number 1505, p. 787, NA, RG 393. (See number 1560, pp. 688-90, NA, RG 396.) Schroeder Collection, NMSRCA.
43. Delano to CIA, LS, June 2, 1873. NA, RG 48. Schroeder Collection, NMSRCA. Lawrence L. Mechan, "A History of the Mescalero Apache Reservation, 1869-1881." (MA Thesis, University of Arizona, 1968.)
44. Quitclaim Deed from Fritz and Murphy to the USA, June 13, 1873. **Deed Book, E-Misc.,** pp. 78-80. Lincoln County Clerk's Office, Carrizozo. (See Dudley to Smith, December 6, 1873, LR, NA, RG 48. Schroeder Collection, NMSRCA.)
45. Lincoln County, **District Court Record,** Criminal Case Numbers 19, 73, 79, 80 and 81. NMSRCA.
46. Preemption patent to L. G. Murphy; **Deed Book, E-Misc.,** pp. 14-6. Transferred to Book C, p. 1. Lincoln County Clerk's Office, Carrizozo. (See Santa Fe County District Court Records, **Citizenship and Naturalization Record Book 1873.** NMSRCA.)
47. Maurice G. Fulton, **History of the Lincoln County War,** (Tucson: University of Arizona Press, 1968), pp. 22-5.

48. **Daily New Mexican,** Santa Fe, NM., December 9, 1873. NMSL.
49. **Daily New Mexican,** Santa Fe, NM., January 9, 1874. NMSL.
50. Brand Book, p. 359. Lincoln County Clerk's Office, Carrizozo.

CHAPTER 4
INTRUDERS

During the Harrell incident, Brady kept his family at home. Sheriff Alex H. Mills did not contact Brady to assist him in capturing the Harrell gang and for some reason, the elected law inforcement authorities were not reliable to prevent such a disaster. But being a spirited citizen, Brady joined the local vigilante committee to protect the community from again being invaded by a violent mob. Obviously, strong leadership to enforce the law was not one of the virtues of Lincoln citizens.

Both before and after the Harrell episode, the citizens of Lincoln County were afraid of becoming involved in arguments, controversies, or disputes. Community involvement was minimal and only a few accepted any responsibility for the survival of Lincoln County. In general, most people did not want to be part of a situation hard to get out of. [1]

There were several good reasons for this frightening atmosphere. Most retail and wholesale establishments in town provided a continuous supply of liquor. Side arms and rifles became the customary habit for men whenever they left home. Moreover, Lincoln County had always been a secluded area of the Territory. Strangers who came into the county were generally looked upon as intruders.

Saloons encouraged a vigorous business and liquor sales increased. Men who frequented the establishments trusted no one, especially strangers. But the aura of distrust was not confined to the local tavern. People throughout the county had adopted a similar attitude toward each other. Possibly the only remaining source of hope for unity remained with family relationships and very close associates.

The courts also found it difficult to prosecute individuals who refused to pay their taxes. Business concerns were reluctant to hand over sizeable amounts of money to anyone without some protest. Because of the enormous size of many cattle ranches, it became almost impossible to arrive at an equitable property assessment. Then, too, ranchers and homesteaders were moving in and settling within the big ranch claims. In many cases, cattle belonging to the newcomers naturally drifted into the larger herds. Accusations of cattle stealing on both sides resulted in gunplay. Many times, especially among the big cattle owners, their law was the law of the hired gun.[2]

Besides the criminal cases assigned to the District Court, there were also numerous civil suits involving individuals and business interests to recover their debts on overdue notes. The cases varied as to the amount of money involved but in some decisions, land became a useful commodity to satisfy the debt. Because lawyers were too scarce and too expensive, many people lost everything they had due to improper defense.

In this atmosphere, Alexander McSween and his wife settled in Lincoln during the spring of 1875. McSween decided to come to the territory for his health and because Lincoln was a promising location to begin the practice of law. The couple soon integrated into frontier life.[3]

McSween set up an office and temporary home in the old courthouse. Then the new barrister hung out his shingle offering capable assistance and knowledge of the law to anyone for a fee, which was usually substantial. When the District Court convened in April McSween was formally admitted to law in the territory and before long he was busy with legal cases that were mostly civil in nature.[4]

By the following year, McSween's business had increased substantially. As early as November 28, 1876, John D. Bail had filed a patent on the tract of land that eventually became the site of McSween's home, office and eventually the Tunstall store. On that same day, Bail sold the parcel to L. G. Murphy. However, Murphy & Co. already had their La Placita Store on the property. In the meantime, Murphy had constructed a new mercantile store across the street. In a warranty deed, Murphy transferred the La Placita property to McSween. By January 1877, McSween had renovated the store and moved into the new facility as his permanent home.[5]

Early in his career in Lincoln, it was said that Alexander McSween expressed concern about the lack of educational and church facilities in the community. Perhaps he felt the town needed a touch of refinement more in tune with his experiences in the East. He was born in Canada and was a Presbyterian. Therefore, he made zealous overtures to the Presbyterian Church to send out missionaries and provide such accomodations. He assured the missionary board that the land had been secured and funds would be made available to establish the church and school.[6]

Meanwhile, as a result of Brady's efforts in the Territorial House of Representatives, the legislature passed the Educational Act of 1872. Lincoln established a school that same year with an attendance of 35 students and increased enrollment every year. The school had one teacher assigned to teach Spanish, reading, writing and arithmetic. The instructor received $50 per month from the county school tax funds to educate the children. Total county educational expenses for the school year were estimated at $1,300.[7]

Another non-sectarian educational facility in the town included a private school that received great support from concerned individuals. The following year Lincoln County residents had selected James H. Farmer, E. Hughs and Serafino Trujillo as members of the first School Commission.[8]

Although McSween was interested in community affairs, he was also aggressive and ambitious and sought to reap a fortune from his adopted section. On several occasions, L. G. Murphy & Co. hired McSween to defend civil cases for the partnership. From all appearances, McSween had become Murphy's attorney. However, McSween often had other clients who paid well even if they were in conflict with his employer.[9]

During this time, Brady was busy with his farm and had very little contact with McSween. And at no time did they meet to discuss community problems. However Brady, as foreman of the Grand Jury in August 1875, became aware of McSween's success in court. During that same month, the Grand Jury indicted William Wilson charged with the murder of Robert Casey, a respected citizen of Lincoln County. Wilson appeared before the District Court in Lincoln for trial where he was found guilty and sentenced to hang. In December, the **Daily New Mexican** furnished a vivid account of the first legal hanging in Lincoln County.[10]

During the early months of 1876, well known outlaws had gathered in substantial numbers from different areas of the country and made their headquarters some 15 or 20 miles below the town. From here they engaged in cattle rustling, horse stealing, pillaging and murder. The citadel, as they called the place, was well fortified with guards to protect the inhabitants and their plunder. All of the known criminals came here to hide from the law. Months later several of the desperados would become part of the groups associated with the disturbing conditions in Lincoln County.[11]

Besides this conclave of thieves, new groups that had been former outlaws elsewhere began moving into Lincoln County. Among the earliest were Juan Gonzales, Jesus Largo and Nica Meras. Younger men also began arriving in the community to escape the law. Jesse (Jessie) Evans who was originally from Missouri drifted into the Mesilla Valley where he met Frank Baker, Jim McDaniels and William Morton. After a brief encounter with the law, the four decided it was time to leave and

50

headed for Lincoln County.[12]

Later, William Bonney alias "Billy the Kid" also sought refuge in the hide-outs of Lincoln. He first came to Santa Fe with his mother, Catherine McCarty, who married William Antrim on March 1, 1873. Bonney was a witness to his mother's marriage where his name had been recorded as Henry McCarty. Shortly after the marriage, the Antrims moved to Silver City, New Mexico. Early in his life, Henry McCarty alias "Billy Antrim" became a wanted criminal. He was arrested for theft and later escaped from jail leaving the territory for Arizona. After some additional confrontations with the law including murder, Henry left Arizona probably living for a time in Mexico and Texas before arriving in Lincoln County sometime in October 1877. After arriving in the community, he assumed the name William H. Bonney while others called him Billy the Kid.[13]

If trouble was beginning to brew in Lincoln County, it was not noticeable to the farmers of the community. Because of the growing interest in agriculture, several prominent citizens of the county met at the county seat to organize the Lincoln County Farmers Club. The officers of the new organization were Lawrence G. Murphy, President; William Brady and Joseph Storms, Vice Presidents; Morris J. Bernstein, Secretary; and Charles Fritz, Treasurer. The club drafted a constitution and by-laws to govern the organization. John Newcomb and Richard Brewer were also present to provide additional assistance to the constitutional committee. Copies of the proceedings were furnished to the Agricultural Department in Washington and the newspapers of the territory for publication. Regular meetings were scheduled each month to communicate and record experiences in matters pertaining to agricultural problems.[14]

Under the new law adopted by the 1876 legislature, the first meeting of the Lincoln County Commissioners was held on March 1, 1876. The three member board consisted of Chairman Paul Dowlin, Florencio Gonzales and Joseph H. Blazer. During the meeting it became evident that a building had to be secured for the April term of court. John B. Wilson offered his home for that purpose to be paid $50 from county funds.[15]

Subsequent commission meetings revealed the issuing of warrants to pay county expenses. The board also redefined the districts of Lincoln County to provide for six voting precincts. During the meeting Florencio Gonzales presented his bill against the county for salary as Probate Judge from October 1, 1875 to March 31, 1876. He had replaced Murphy who resigned in September 1875. Sheriff Saturnino Baca also presented his bill for services rendered. Baca had been appointed as the sheriff of the county by Governor Giddings when Alexander Mills was removed from office.[16]

In August 1876, L. G. Murphy and William Brady were nominated and elected to represent the Democratic party from Lincoln County in the Territorial Convention in Santa Fe later that month. Also, Brady had been traveling around the county to register voters for the November general election. McSween was also elected as a delegate to the Republican Convention to be held in Santa Fe and authorized to recruit new membership for the party. There is no doubt that this occasion gave both men an opportunity to meet and exchange their party philosophy. Although a Canadian, McSween had registered to vote in 1875.[17]

At the general election held in November, the voters had an opportunity to select some responsible citizen for every elected office in the county. The voters elected William Dowlin, Francisco Romero y Luera and Juan Patron as their new county commissioners. Florencio Gonzales was unopposed for the office of Probate Judge. The electorate chose William Brady as sheriff by a substantial margin over the incumbent Saturnino Baca and office hopeful Elisha Dow. L. G. Murphy did not vote for Brady but instead, cast his ballot for Sheriff Baca.[18]

The reason Murphy gave his support to Baca will probably always remain a mystery. It might safely be assumed that Murphy felt he had a better chance to keep control of county business with Baca as sheriff rather than Brady. Murphy was no longer Probate Judge. Furthermore, Murphy had previously recommended to the governor to have Baca appointed to the sheriff's post in 1875.[19]

Historians have written that Brady was a "Murphy henchman" and took his orders from the man who had been responsible for placing him in office. But Murphy never placed Brady in any office. As friends and kinsmen, they were from similar backgrounds and raised in the same country. However, Brady's childhood development combined with his military training supported his continuing belief that law and order was the motivating force for a stable community. His posture toward community living was probably in conflict not only with Murphy, but with other influential members of the community. Because of their association, some members of the town believed that the new sheriff had influence with the so-called "Santa Fe Ring." But this has never been proven conclusively.[20]

For Justice of the Peace in Precinct 1, the voters chose James H. Farmer. Shortly after the election, Farmer resigned stating that personal commitments and distance to Lincoln prohibited him from carrying on the duties of his elected office. The County Commissioners then

52

appointed John B. Wilson to be the new Justice of the Peace. Several months later Governor Axtell, while on an official visit in Lincoln to determine the cause of violence in the community, removed Wilson as Justice of the Peace. Axtell informed the County Commissioners that they had no authority to appoint elected officials especially those officials whose office is prescribed by law.[21]

According to the governor, the law describing the office of Justice of the Peace had not been amended by the County Commissioners Act of 1876. Furthermore, the appointment clause in the act was in direct violation of the Organic Law established by congress. The Organic Act that established New Mexico as a Territory of the United States provided for all county officials to be elected. During the administration of Governor Lew. Wallace, a similar incident occurred in Rio Arriba County. Wallace removed him from office.[22]

Without exception each of the offices of Probate Judge and Sheriff were also prescribed by law. Obviously, congressional as well as territorial authority were encroaching on the newly formed commission status. It would be some time before the commissioners realized that their ordinances were not allowed to be in conflict with high constituted authority.[23]

Late in 1876, on one of his many trips to Santa Fe, Alexander McSween became acquainted with an Englishman, John Henry Tunstall. Saturnino Baca and Juan Patron had also made the trip to Santa Fe with McSween to purchase supplies and equipment. It was at this time Tunstall made known to McSween his scheme to acquire vast acres of land in the territory, stock it with cattle and become one of the wealthy tenants in New Mexico. Tunstall had been well informed on land deals by his friends in California.[24]

John Henry Tunstall was born March 6, 1853, in the county of Middlesex northwest of London, England. His father, John Partridge Tunstall, was the manager of a shipping firm in London. He was also in partnership with John Hubert Turner and Henry Beeton who owned a wholesale and retail business in Victoria, Canada. His son, John, was sent to Victoria to help manage the store.[25]

After several months of difficulty with the business, Tunstall became bored with the firm. In February 1876, Tunstall wrote his family about leaving Victoria, Canada for New Mexico. Tunstall spoke of his meeting with an attorney, R. Guy McLellan, who provided him with legal advice on how to acquire government land and receive clear title to the property. Citizens of the United States would have to be hired to apply for title to the land under the Preemption Act. Then a deed of conveyance would be given to Tunstall without having to show proof of citizenship. Then camps would be set up along the river wherever he settled to prevent intending settlers from locating where they might be in Tunstall's way. He said that the politics were in the hands of a ring who controlled things as they liked. This was a problem that would have to be managed carefully. [26]

On another occasion, Tunstall discussed at some length his feelings for the Spanish women who apparently held no charms for him. One evening he attended a social gathering in California and met several Spanish ladies. He even danced with one of the young women who was attending the San Jose Ladies Academy. But he would never be tempted to marry any of them. He said: "Their imperfections lie in their ignorance of economy, love of display which degrades their husbands." While he considered the Spanish to be uncivilized and irresponsible, it later became necessary for Tunstall to use the Spanish people to accomplish his land scheme in Lincoln County. [27]

Through all of his planning and scheming Tunstall was setting up his father. He looked forward to the day the Victoria business would fail. Then J. P. Tunstall would recover his share of the profits and invest it in New Mexico. He and his father together could buy two or three deeds, stock part of the property with cattle, get it on a paying basis, then mortgage the other tracts at the lowest possible rate of interest to be in a financial position to invest in additional tracts of land. [28]

Tunstall arrived in Santa Fe in August 1876, and immediately secured a room at the Herlow Hotel located on San Francisco Street. He chose this "very second rate hotel," as he called it because the place was usually frequented by individuals who could help him increase his business knowledge about New Mexico without their knowing his intentions. He also met Robert W. Widenmann there. Over the next few months, Widenmann was to play an important role in the troubled conditions in Lincoln County. McSween had registered at the hotel where both he and Tunstall made plans to become wealthy landowners in the territory. It was McSween who convinced Tunstall to settle in Lincoln County. [29]

Later, when the wagons were finally loaded, Tunstall made arrangements to return to Lincoln with Juan Patron. Saturnino Baca and Alexander McSween occupied the second wagon and the four of them headed south arriving in Lincoln on November 7, 1876. This chance meeting between McSween and Tunstall was to foster a very close alliance. McSween was jealous of Murphy's economic and political power and intended to find a way to replace him.

Tunstall came from a wealthy English family and was eager to make a fortune in the expanding Southwest. He often wrote home bragging to his family about his machinations. McSween would use Tunstall's financial backing to secure the power he desired. Tunstall wanted to control Lincoln County and he intended to acquire land with illegal manipulations of the law.

CHAPTER 4
NOTES

1. William A. Keleher, **Violence in Lincoln County,** (Albuquerque: University of New Mexico Press, 1957), pp. 14-5.
2. Lincoln County, **District Court Records** (1873-1879.) NMSRCA.
3. Victor Westphall, **Thomas Benton Catron and his Era,** (Tucson: University of Arizona Press, 1973), p. 77.
4. Keleher, **Lincoln County,** pp. 54-5.
5. Lincoln County Records, **Patent Book F,** pp. 342-43; **Contract Book B,** pp. 24-5; and **Deed Book B,** pp. 2-9. Clerk's Office, Lincoln County Courthouse, Carrizozo.
6. Lincoln County Records, **Deed Book B,** pp. 50-3. Clerk's Office, Lincoln County Courthouse, Carrizozo.
7. Territory of New Mexico, **Report of W. G. Ritch, Secretary of New Mexico to the Commissioner of Education Washington, D.C.** (December 31, 1873) NMSRCA. (See **Arizona and the West,** University of Arizona Press, Vol. 26, No. 2, 1984. "The Public School Debate in New Mexico 1850-1891," by Dianna Everett, pp. 109-11.
8. Lincoln County, **Poll Book of Elections 1873.** NMSRCA.
9. Lincoln County, **District Court Record Book** (1873-1878). NMSRCA.
10. **Daily New Mexican,** December 21, 1875. NMSL. (Also see court case #160, Lincoln County, **District Court Record Book** [1873-1879.] NMSRCA.)
11. Fulton, **Lincoln County War,** pp. 65-6.
12. Ibid., pp. 67-8.
13. Santa Fe County Records, **Marriage Record Book** (1863-1899), p. 35a. NMSRCA. (See James A. Shinkle, **Robert Casey and the Ranch on the Rio Hondo,** (Roswell: Hall-Poorbaugh Press, Inc., 1970), pp. 101-106.
14. **Weekly New Mexican,** January 2, 1876. NMSL.
15. Territory of New Mexico, **General Laws of New Mexico,** (Prince, 1882); County Commissioners Act of 1876, Art. 18, Ch. 43. pp. 222-33. NMSRCA. (Lincoln County Records, **Commissioners Record Book** (1876-1879), pp. 1-4. Clerk's Of-

fice, Lincoln County Courthouse, Carrizozo.)

16. Lincoln County Records, **Commissioners Record Book** (1876-1879), pp. 15-20. Clerk's Office, Lincoln County Courthouse, Carrizozo.

17. Lincoln County, **Voter Registrations** (1875 through 1877) NMSRCA.

18. Lincoln County, **Poll Book of Elections** (1875 and 1876) NMSRCA.

19. **Executive Record** (1867-1882), p. 198. NMSRCA.
   Governor Axtell ordered an election to be held in Lincoln County on September 25, 1875 to fill vacancies that occurred as a result of resignations and removal from office. Those elected would serve until the next general election to be held in November 1876. NMSRCA.

20. Fulton, **Lincoln County War**, p. 71.

21. Lincoln County Records, **Commissioners Record Book** (1876-1879), p. 25. Clerk's Office, Lincoln County Courthouse, Carrizozo.

22. Territory of New Mexico, **General Laws of New Mexico.** (Prince, 1882); Act of 1876, **Vacancy in the Office of Justice of the Peace**; Art. 11, Ch. 22, Sec. 4, p. 85. (**Executive Record**, LS, 1878-1885. TANM Roll #99, Frame 101.) NMSRCA.

23. Territory of New Mexico, **General Laws of New Mexico.** (Prince, 1882); Act of 1876, **Vacancy in the Office of Probate Judge**; Art. 11, Ch. 21, Sec. 2, p. 80. **Vacancy in the Office of Sheriff**; Art. 59, Ch. 94, Sec. 8, p. 532. NMSRCA.

24. J. H. Tunstall to J. P. Tunstall, (February 3, 1876). Fulton Papers, Box 14; Special Collections, University of Arizona Library, Tucson.

25. Frederick W. Nolan, **The Life and Death of John Henry Tunstall**, (Albuquerque: The University of New Mexico Press), p. 9. (See Keleher, **Lincoln County**, p. 105.)

26. J. H. Tunstall to My Much Beloved Father, (June 26, 1876). Fulton Papers, Box 14; Special Collections, University of Arizona Library, Tucson.

27. J. H. Tunstall to My Much Beloved Governor, (July 15, 1876). Fulton Papers, Box 14; Special Collections, University of Arizona Library, Tucson.

28. J. H. Tunstall to My Much Beloved Father, (August 4, 1876). Fulton Papers, Box 14; Special Collections, University of Arizona Library, Tucson.

29. Nolan, **John Henry Tunstall**, p. 108.

CHAPTER 5
CONTRAVENTION

When William Brady finally secured full title to his 320 acres of land at Walnut Grove he continued to improve the farm. In the fall of 1875, with the help of neighbors and some hired hands, the large barn north of Brady's home was completed. Recent additions to the Brady family required the building of two more rooms onto the house. And pasture lands were fenced off to accomodate the increasing cattle herd. The land south of the Brady home contained the most fertile soil on the farm. This land, situated on the banks of the Rio Bonito, gave Brady the opportunity to raise a variety of crops including a lush vineyard.[1]

By early 1876, a situation evolved in Lincoln which at the time seemed relatively unimportant. Emil Fritz, in partnership with Murphy & Co., left the country and returned to Germany where he died in 1874. It was assumed that he left a will designating his estate to the remaining members of his family. But after several unsuccessful attempts to locate the will, it was decided to administer his estate based on the probability that Fritz died intestate and thus his assets would be distributed to the surviving relatives in accordance with New Mexico Law.[2]

Fritz was survived by his father who lived in Germany and by a younger brother and sister, Charles Philip Frederick Fritz and Emilie Fritz Scholand, both of whom lived in Lincoln County. Emilie Fritz had married William Scholand from whom she was divorced in April of 1876. Custody of their two children was granted to Mrs. Scholand. In December of 1876, Emilie and her two children left Lincoln and settled in Silver City, Dona Ana County, New Mexico. Within two years, she and her family moved to Clifton, Apache County, Arizona Territory. Sometime later she met and married David Abraham who owned a small ranch near town.[3]

In April 1876, the court appointed William Brady to be the administrator of the Fritz estate. Involved with the estate was an insurance policy issued by the Merchants Life Insurance Company of New York City on the life of Emil Fritz in the amount of $10,000. Collecting on the policy proved to be exceedingly difficult because the company had declared bankruptcy. To further complicate matters, the Spiegelberg Brothers of Santa Fe claimed that Fritz had assigned the policy to them as security for a debt. Murphy also filed a claim against the policy stating that Fritz owed the firm several thousand dollars. However, the court disallowed the case because Murphy was unable to show cause for the claim.[4]

Because of the complexity of the problem, the Probate Judge, Florencio Gonzales, authorized Brady to obtain assistance in collecting on the policy. The court appointed Alexander McSween as counsel. McSween, of course, continued in his employment as the attorney for Murphy & Co. until August 1876.[5]

During the following months, Brady must have become very concerned about the immense problems surrounding the arduous task of administering the estate of Emil Fritz. Perhaps he became aware of the methods that were being used to collect the insurance money. In August, Brady was elected as a delegate from Lincoln County to the Democratic Convention in Santa Fe. When he returned Brady began his campaign for sheriff. And because of the possibility of a conflict of interest, then resigned as administrator of the Fritz estate on September 19, 1876.[6]

The court appointed Emilie Scholand and Charles Fritz to succeed him and furnished a $10,000 surety bond. The bondsmen were James J. Dolan and Alexander A. McSween who had been retained as counsel by the new administrators. The court also authorized Levi Spiegelberg of New York City to collect the money on the Fritz estate and deliver the funds to the Probate Court in Lincoln.[7]

In November 1876, McSween was in Santa Fe and perhaps unaware of the transaction taking place in New York. When he returned to Lincoln the court informed McSween about the new development in the case. McSween immediately prepared his traveling agenda and began a hasty trip to St. Louis to consult some bankers. After opening an account with the Merchant's National Bank of St. Louis, McSween then headed for New York hoping to collect the money on the Fritz insurance policy. In December, McSween returned to Lincoln and informed the administrators, Emilie Scholand and Charles Fritz, that it would be months before the insurance money would be paid. His ostensible purpose for the trip was securing the $10,000 for the heirs of Emil Fritz. But McSween neglected to tell them that arrangements were already being made to have the money deposited in his own bank account in St. Louis.[8]

Several months went by and no insurance money appeared. As far as Emilie Scholand and Charles Fritz were concerned, the proceeds of the estate were still with Donnell, Lawson & Co., the bankers in New York City. The firm had been designated as the receiver of the defunct insurance company. Judge Gonzales wrote a letter on behalf of the administrators instructing the bank to forward the money to the First National Bank of Santa Fe to the credit of Charles Fritz. But the funds were secretly tucked away in McSween's bank in St. Louis.[9]

In July 1877, through some clever manipulations of the law, McSween petitioned the court requesting that both Emilie Scholand and Charles Fritz give an account of their administration. He also charged that Mrs. Scholand had not been in the county to perform her duties as administratrix of the estate and that Charles Fritz had not followed his instructions. In another accusation, McSween declared that both heirs were incompetent to administer assets of the estate. Since he had found a legal method to prevent court action on the insurance money, it may safely be assumed that McSween had intended to embezzle the funds from the Fritz estate.[10]

While the courts and the administrators of the insurance claim were left in a state of confusion, Tunstall and McSween were making future plans. They decided to spend some time touring the county in search of unoccupied land including property that had been acquired by improper title. Tunstall used McSween to advise him on the most promising ranch land and to recommend a method to take possession. During this time, Robert Widenmann arrived in Lincoln and immediately contacted John Tunstall. Later this casual association was to foster a close relationship.[11]

Meanwhile Brady attended to his own ranch and performed the duties assigned to him as sheriff of the county. Although Tunstall was secretive about his schemes, Brady should have become suspicious of Tunstall's motives in traveling around the country especially with McSween as a companion. Rumors of huge investments being considered by the Tunstall and McSween combination fortified Brady's distrust. Further concerns were expressed by the Lincoln County citizenry when Tunstall purchased horses and cattle from John Chisum and began his business venture on what was considered open range near the Rio Feliz. Moreover, Tunstall and Chisum made frequent trips to the Oklahoma Territory where Tunstall eventually purchased horses. The animals were to be placed on the Chisum South Spring Ranch near Roswell until Tunstall could locate them on permanent pasture land in Lincoln County.[12]

It is likely that Brady never forgot the methods used by the English to confiscate property and force the Irish to become tenants on their own land. He did not intend this type of environment to exist in the county. [13]

On March 14, 1877, L. G. Murphy withdrew his name from the co-partnership of Murphy & Co. Murphy then sold his interest in the firm to James J. Dolan and John H. Riley under the partnership of Jas. J. Dolan & Co. Murphy left Lincoln and returned to his ranch near Carrizozo, New Mexico. During the same month, the federal government establish-ed the Desert Land Act. The program had been designed to encourage settlers to areas where irrigation was necessary to produce agricultural crops. But the Englishman had no interest in agriculture and this turn of events would have far reaching concerns for Tunstall. [14]

Since the new federal program encouraged settlers, Tunstall kept up the pressure on his father to send more money. He assured his father that everything had been going well for him. "I have a presentment that I shall 'not' get killed by I 'shall live' to accomplish my schemes and give those pets 'such a time as will make their heads swim' (as we say on the frontier)." Although he had secured a small herd of cattle, Tunstall had his eye on other stock in Lincoln County.

Tunstall told his father that all the officials from the president downward were incompetent and that laws governing American society fostered this state of affairs. He said New Mexico was controlled by a ring composed of two or three lawyers. Later, Tunstall's plan for Lincoln included the establishment of his own "ring" to keep the community divided.

While the citizens were figting among themselves, Tunstall's work proceeded unnoticed. With the aid of his father's money, Tunstall intend-ed to raise cattle near the Casey Mill and Ranch located at the con-fluence of the Rio Hondo and the Rio Feliz where he could control the water supply. [15]

Tunstall found that some wealthy individuals were looking into the possibility of settling in the immediate vicinity of the Rio Feliz and ac-quiring land under the Desert Land Act. This development frustrated Tunstall who prepared to initiate his "bold swift policy." In view of the circumstances, he intended to run a herd of cattle in the area to keep them from cultivating the land. He selected the best locations, establish-ed cow camps, and employed men who would claim they owned the property. [16]

Toward the end of March, J. P. Tunstall sent a short letter announc-ing the second cash installment of 1,000 pounds ($4,812) to his son in Lincoln. He promised the third cash advance in April. The first draft was sent while Tunstall was in Santa Fe. [17]

The following month, Tunstall promptly employed Godfrey Gauss as the cook, John Middleton as the ranch hand and Richard Brewer as the ranch foreman (who was said to own a ranch in the Hondo Valley north of the Rio Feliz). These employees then became the nucleus of Tunstall's ranching business. Once the hiring had been completed Tunstall began his trip back east and opened an account with the Merchants' National Bank of St. Louis. When the money from England arrived in St. Louis, Tunstall immediately prepared a draft of $5,142.82 to be credited to the personal account of A. A. McSween, First National Bank of Santa Fe. [18]

Further evidence of McSween's bulging personal bank account was noted in the First National of Santa Fe records. On July 19, 1877, another Tunstall draft for $2,000 had been deposited to A. A. McSween. [19]

Then in August and again in October, two additional deposits of $1,000 in gold were made to that same account from Boatmans Exchange and Savings Bank of Kansas City, Missouri. From a total of $14,436 John Tunstall received from his father, $9,142.82 had been deposited to the account of Alexander A. McSween, First National Bank of Santa Fe. Tunstall and McSween had discussed a joint venture in a mercantile store and bank in Lincoln. As a result, there were more than 60 checks showing payments to various merchants who furnished materials to construct the building and provide the supplies for the store. But it is hard to know what happened to the balance of the money since McSween's ledger also identifies his personal funds. [20]

In August, the Tunstall-McSween Mercantile Store opened for business. On the same premises, Tunstall, McSween and John Chisum, as president, established the Lincoln County Bank. [21]

During this episode, Tunstall never told his father about building the store, establishing a bank and furnishing materials to establish camps in the vicinity of his chosen ranch land. But he did say everything in New Mexico is worked by a ring. "There is the Indian Ring, the Political Ring, the Legal Ring, the Roman Catholic Ring, the Horse Thieves Ring, the Cattle Ring and half dozen other rings. Now to make things stick to do any good it is necessary to either get into a ring or make one for yourself. I am working at present making a ring and I have succeeded admirably so far." Tunstall spoke with confidence that he could break up any ring. "I can see false economy in the business of a rancher at a glance and if so minded, can make him stiffen and roach his back like a mule and buck through the ring that is using him and that complaint is very catching amongst the class." He intended to confine his operations to Lincoln County and get half of every dollar that was made in the county by anyone. [22]

At this time, Tunstall's followers did not know that the bottom line in their operations was the plan to "skim the milk" from the citizens. But Tunstall had one specific problem concerning the inhabitants: to make them believe he was an honest, concerned individual who was settling in Lincoln not only because he loved the country, but to help the citizens of Lincoln to lead a more productive life. However, Tunstall convinced his father that McSween could not cause any trouble. "I believe I have him [McSween] in such a shape that he can't slide back a single point." [23]

By October 1877, everyone in Lincoln was aware of the immediate plans of Tunstall and McSween. But Tunstall's mercantile store in town certainly hid from view the underlying intentions of the new partnership. Moreover, suspicious looking characters infiltrated Lincoln and headed for the open range near the Rio Feliz. Many of them were hired by Tunstall who anticipated an expansion in the cattle business. This particular element in association with Tunstall and McSween was seen moving about the county much to the displeasure of Sheriff Brady and the citizenry. [24]

By this time, Brady had cause to believe that the Tunstall-McSween operation was gearing-up for further exploitation of the community. Brady's land had been secured by legal title. But there were many families living in the area who did not have a patent to their property. Some were squatters. In many cases, the land had been acquired by a quitclaim deed which was not sufficient to clear title.

As Tunstall was tightening his grip on Lincoln County, Brady was busy attending to official duties. Early in May, Brady arrested James Dolan who had shot and killed one of his employees, Hilario Jaramillo, in self-defense. Testimony revealed that Dolan had apparently told the truth. Charges against Dolan were dismissed by the court.

In another incident, Paul Dowlin had been murdered by a former employee, Jerry Dillon. Within a few hours Sheriff Brady mustered a posse, secured a warrant and went after the criminal. The murderer's trail led Brady and his posse eastward where Dillon escaped to Texas and was never heard from again. Dowlin was an early resident of Lincoln and owned several ranches, mills and considerable property in the area. [25]

In May 1877, a well-known desperado, Frank Freeman, formerly of Alabama, appeared in town. Freeman had been in the vicinity the previous year and had settled on public land on the Upper Penasco near the land claimed by Tunstall. Freeman built living quarters and a corral on the property. Later, Tunstall made arrangements with Freeman to purchase the buildings for a few hundred dollars before he left. [26]

Besides the money offered, there must have been other promises made to Freeman for him to vacate the premises so easily. Apparently, the "Tunstall crowd" had not kept their word. On August 6, 1877, John Chisum was visiting in the McSween home in Lincoln. When Freeman arrived he and Charles Bowdre, who it seems squatted on some land on the Ruidoso, paid a visit to McSween demanding that Chisum step outside. When he refused they began shooting. [27]

Freeman then entered a nearby restaurant where he shot and killed a sergeant from Fort Stanton. Sheriff Brady and a posse arrested Freeman and turned him over to the soldiers from the fort. While under military escort to Fort Stanton, Freeman managed to escape and later joined a band of cattle rustlers and thieves who were located on the Rio Ruidoso. Brady and his posse, together with a detachment from Fort Stanton, surrounded the hideout. After several exchanges of gunfire, most of the gang surrendered except for Freeman, who was killed while attempting to escape. Charles Bowdre was able to elude his captors. [28]

Meanwhile, Tunstall realized another opportunity to acquire additional property now that Bowdre left his land unprotected. He also expressed an interest in the Post tradership at Fort Stanton that was to become vacant within a few months. He told his father about the value of his new schemes. "Unless you were here, you could never understand all these things about the army and Indian contracts, the post tradership, the cattle range and the way one range secures the other, and the ranches, and the water rights, and the mills, and the squatters and a thousand other corners that have to be tucked up and worked and 'then don't the grist just come in Stranger? No, I guess not!' as a Yankee would say and wink with his right eye and squirt some tobacco juice out of the left side of his mouth." [29]

During the early months of 1877, property owners in Lincoln County were required by law to render property taxes. By May, the assessment rolls were completed and certified by Juan Patron, Chairman, Board of County Commissioners. John Chisum had previously sold out his ranch holdings to R. D. Hunter and A. G. Evans of Kansas City, Missiouri. Therefore, most of the county taxes were to be paid by the following businesses and individuals: Robert D. Hunter, $3,059.75; Jas. J. Dolan & Co., $336.65; Paul Dowlin Co. Bros., $282.44; Lawrence G. Murphy, $175.24; J. H. Blazer, $119.05; Ellen E. Casey (Estate), $116.21; C. Coghlan, $107.35; and A. A. McSween, $105.95. Taxes to be paid by the remaining proeprty owners amounted to less than $30 each. The total assessment for tax purposes in Lincoln County amounted to $5,248.06. [30]

After the taxes were paid, the county commission was responsible for separating the funds into three distinct agencies of government. Each agency then was to receive a percentage of the tax; for the territory, $1,968.02½ or 37.5%; for the county, $1,968.02½ or 37.5%; and for the support of schools $1,312.01 or 25% totaling $5,248.06. The county sheriff is the ex-officio tax collector and authorized by the county commission to collect the property taxes. License fees amounting to $168.75 or 1877 were paid directly to the commission.[31]

Toward the end of May 1877, Jas. J. Dolan & Co. successfully obtained a civil judgement against the Casey family. The suit included some 400 head of cattle to liquidate a debt owed to the firm. The court ordered Brady to seize the cattle and to hold a sheriff's auction to dispose of the animals. The money received from the auction had to be returned to the court and then remitted to James Dolan.

Brady posted the appropriate 30-day auction notice in several convenient places around town. Once Tunstall was informed of the auction, he wrote to his father explaining the excellent prospects to purchase several hundred head of cattle and place them on an open range north of the Rio Feliz. In the letter, Tunstall estimated that he could purchase the cattle for less than $4 per head.[32]

Since the auction was to be held in June, Tunstall made an immediate commitment and authorized Alexander McSween to put in a bid for the steers. In order for McSween to do this he needed some assurance that Tunstall would have the funds available upon receipt of the cattle. Therefore, on July 2, 1877, McSween secured check #17 from John H. Tunstall for $2,000 on the Merchants' National Bank of St. Louis and made payable to the account of A. A. McSween Esq., First National Bank of Santa Fe.[33]

Bids were made by interested parties but most of them recognized the fact that Tunstall was financially supported by large sums of money from England. Because of the funding assistance from home, Tunstall's emissary offered the highest bid for the cattle. Then on July 31, 1877, McSween executed his check #300 for the Casey cattle in the amount of $1,545.13. The check was made out to the order of William Brady, Sheriff and Ex-officio Tax Collector Lincoln County, New Mexico. This would seem appropriate since Brady was the legally authorized collector of county funds. After the auction, Brady endorsed the check and turned if over to the court. The court approved the check and then completed its transaction by remitting check #300 to James Dolan. The check represented full payment on the civil suit brought by Dolan against the Caseys.[34]

On August 23rd as full payment for the cattle, check #300 had been processed through the First National Bank of Santa Fe showing a debit to McSween's account for $1,545.13. There is one important question regarding this transaction that has never been answered. Where is the $454.87 remaining from the $2,000 check for cattle paid to McSween by John Henry Tunstall? There seems to be no available evidence that the balance had ever been returned to McSween's benefactor. Evidently the money had been absorbed in McSween's personal account.[35]

After the auction and the financial transactions were completed in July, Brady began the hard task of collecting property taxes. For the next several months, he performed his job admirably under very trying circumstances. Many property owners simply refused to pay on time and this made it difficult for Brady to complete his schedule. Although he was several weeks late, he finally managed to collect the taxes and early in January 1878, submitted the funds to the county commission who by law must certify the account and remit the tax due to the Territorial Treasurer in Santa Fe.[36]

The Lincoln County Commission sanctioned Brady's tax account verifying $1,968.02½, and approved license fees of $168.75 for the territorial treasury. The remaining $3,280.03½ was retained for county and school expenses. On January 8, 1878, the Territorial Treasurer entered the Lincoln County tax into his journal. On January 9th, a report from the treasurer's office certifying the funds had been forwarded to the Territorial Auditor who approved the account including license fees totaling $2,136.77½.[37]

However, in his speech to the Territorial Assembly on January 8, 1878, Governor Axtell made reference to the Auditor's statement of the previous week that "the present sheriff of Lincoln County has paid nothing during his present term of office." Unfortunately the governor was not properly informed and his statement reflects the poor communication between territorial officials. Shortly thereafter, however, Antonio Ortiz y Salazar of the Territorial Treasurer's Office, corrected the governor's error.[38]

It is interesting to note that five months after check #300 for $1,545.13 had been charged to the McSween account for cattle, and the county taxes paid in proper form, Tunstall sent a letter to the Mesilla **Independent** dated January 18, 1878, accusing Sheriff Brady of misappropriating county tax funds. He stated that A. A. McSween paid over $1,500 in taxes by check on the First National Bank of Santa Fe. But Tunstall neglected to mention that the money ($1,545.13) represented the amount bid by McSween for the Casey cattle. Furthermore, the **In-**

dependent was owned and operated by one of McSween's cronies, Albert J. Fountain & Associates.[39]

It might easily be said that Tunstall was not completely familiar with the tax laws and procedures of New Mexico. But more specifically, Brady was now getting close to Tunstall's activities. Tunstall probably wrote the news item in an attempt to divert attention from his clandestine business operation. In several letters to his family in England, Tunstall stated that he would work his schemes in such a way "to make their heads swim." Since he did not mention anyone in particular, Tunstall must have been referring to everyone in Lincoln County.

Since it was McSween who gave Brady the check for the cattle, it is strange that he did not voice his opinion to the newspaper or the court. He was one of the best lawyers in Lincoln and knew his options. Yet he filed no charges against Sheriff Brady. At the time, McSween was unwilling to make any statement about Brady, about the check, or even comment about the county tax money. For obvious reasons, McSween would not disclose that he had paid the tax money including a delinquent statement, July 28, 1877, from his personal account. Later, Dolan wrote a letter to the same newspaper stating that "Sheriff Brady can show clean receipts from the Territorial Treasurer for his account."[40]

From the 1878 Territorial Treasurer's record, including local documents, it is evident that Brady complied with the law. Furthermore, the statements in the newspapers clearly demonstrate that Dolan and Tunstall were either uninformed on specific procedures to remit tax money to the Territorial government in Santa Fe, or it was just a plain act of intimidation. Both newspaper articles, therefore, suggest the continuance of a personal feud between the English-Scotch combination and the Irish contingency that has been evident since the arrival of John Henry Tunstall and his close alliance with Alexander A. McSween.[41]

During the final months of 1877, Brady's official duties covered a wide range. He continued his tour of the county to collect some remaining property taxes. At the same time, he made necessary preparations for the October term of court. Combined with his other duties as county peace officer, Brady was responsible for the citizens of Lincoln who had been selected to serve on the grand and petit juries. As the court bailiff, the sheriff had to be in attendance each day of the session.[42]

In order to be in court, Brady hired some farm hands to help with the fall harvest. One of his new employees was William Bonney. The young drifter was tired, hungry and needed a place to stay. Brady felt sorry for Billy and gave him a job. Apparently Bonney spent only a few days at the farm and then decided to work at a store in town. Later he found employment as a cowboy working for L. G. Murphy. After a short stay on the Carrizozo Ranch, Billy decided to leave the area stopping at farms and ranches along the way until he reached the Coe farm south of Dowlin's Mill. From here, Billy made his way to the Beckwith Ranch at Seven Rivers.[43]

In the meantime, Tunstall was busy in St. Louis making arrangements to supply his new mercantile store with an assortment of eastern goods. The letter of credit from England had been received at the Merchants' National Bank of St. Louis to ensure the success of his enterprise. Wholesale merchants in New Mexico demanded cash and therefore refused to extend credit on Tunstall's signature. His operation was delayed by the "contrariety of some men who needed killing very badly and live in Lincoln."[44]

It seems strange that Tunstall spent so much time building his store and supplying it with all sorts of merchandise. Tunstall had left Victoria, Canada because he detested this very kind of enterprise. As a matter of fact Tunstall looked forward to the day the Victoria business would fail. Merchandising had not been his mission or objective for Lincoln County. Tunstall always wanted either to raise sheep or cattle and eventually own land. He had specific plans for his business operations in Lincoln County so the new store would be used simply as a front to conduct his land grab schemes.

In order for these schemes to be successful, Tunstall recruited citizens who were loyal to him and to his programs. He provided money for citizens to purchase government land and these individuals became tenants on their property. Then contract agreements would have to be made with the loyalists giving Tunstall a legal title to the land. The new bank, Tunstall's lending institution, had been designed to make loans available to anyone in the county. If Tunstall's new found tenants were ever in default to either the bank or the store, then Tunstall had the legal right to bring a suit against them in court.[45]

Besides his land scheme Tunstall perceived the bright prospects of controlling the money flow in Lincoln. Everyone had to be paid in government script which required several days to have transferred into United States currency. Tunstall intended to purchase the script from the local citizens at two-thirds of its value, and return the script to the government exchange office and make a huge profit.[46]

During the final months of 1877, activities in the county increased. Farmers and ranchers were busy with the fall harvest and rounding up the cattle. Brady moved about the county collecting property taxes. And, the Tunstall-McSween cattle and land business began to take shape.

Rumors of new land acquisitions by the business association generated a feeling of uneasiness among the small ranchers and farmers. Later, they expressed their concerns to the sheriff. But since neither Tunstall nor McSween were violating any laws, Sheriff Brady could not interfere.[47]

As a law enforcement officer, Brady was aware of the covert activities by Tunstall & Co. that could eventually affect the entire county. But he would have to handle the situation carefully as Tunstall's operations were cleverly devised. Brady had to furnish proof that the Englishman and his cohorts planned to deceive the citizenry by manipulating land contracts and eventually controlling the flow of goods. This would leave Tunstall & Co. free to direct the economic affairs in Lincoln County.

Friendships were being sacrificed and special interest groups were increasingly hostile toward one another. Under these conditions Tunstall made a pretense of being a sociable individual and fooled most of the people by his genteel manner. But his true colors were shown by his statements: "I would not give a red cent for any Mexican I have ever seen."[48]

Brady now had to be more careful so that peace could be maintained. But he knew about certain matters that needed to be brought into the open. Evidence seemed to show that Tunstall hired men of questionable character who were willing and able to protect his interests. Land and money were promised. Yet Tunstall's claim to several thousand acres of land in Lincoln County had never been recorded on the property tax rolls.[49]

By the end of September, a new jail with an adjoining home for the jailer was completed by the contractor, George W. Peppin. On October 2, 1877, the County Commissioners appointed Saturnino Baca, Sheriff William Brady and John B. Wilson to inspect the facilities. Total cost of the jail and home amounted to $1,700 which was subsequently paid by the County Commission.[50]

Midway through the month of September, Jesse Evans and his gang went on a rampage stealing cattle including two horses and a pair of mules from the Tunstall spread near the Rio Feliz. In the meantime, Tunstall was in Trinidad, Colorado, purchasing additional supplies for his new store.

Sheriff Brady, who was attending court, was informed of the theft and he immediately deputized Richard Brewer and several other citizens to apprehend the criminals and return the stolen horses and cattle. Jesse Evans, Frank Baker, Tom Hill, and George Davis were responsible for the act. They took the cattle and horses to Sheds Ranch near the San Agustin Pass in the San Andres Mountains. Brewer and the posse overtook the desperados at Sheds Ranch where Brewer demanded release of the stolen horses. Evans refused stating he would return only Brewer's horses and keep the ones that belonged to Tunstall. Apparently Brewer was not interested in the cattle. The situation reached an impasse and Brewer and his posse, without making any arrests, returned to Lincoln.[51]

Within a few days, the sheriff received word that the thieves had been seen in the vicinity of Beckwith's ranch at Seven Rivers. Brady then recruited some local citizens, formed a posse and again went after the criminals. Richard Brewer joined this posse even though he demonstrated poor leadership before. After some resistance, the sheriff arrested four members of the gang and escorted them to Lincoln depositing them in the county jail. Some of the animals were located and returned to their owners.[52]

The episode at Seven Rivers for the most part indicated that the community did not intend to take part in the affairs of Lincoln. They had no intention of being allied with any faction causing trouble in the county. In most cases, the Seven Rivers community banded together to defend themselves against a common enemy.[53]

Tunstall then appeared to visit with the Evans gang in jail. The discussion led to the theft of Tunstall's horses and mules and he wanted to know where the animals were located and when Jesse planned to return them. Evans said he would return all of Tunstall's animals when he (Jesse) got out of jail. Later, Tunstall sent Jesse a promised bottle of whiskey.[54]

The following day, Brewer and Tunstall went to the jail for another conference. The criminals were outside exercising which gave them ample time for conversation. Most of the discussion revolved around the stolen horses and business matters. Finally Jesse and the boys were ordered inside the jail but Jesse asked Brewer and Tunstall to visit a little longer to "talk over matters and things."[55]

For this they needed the sheriff's approval. But Brady refused. "He is an Irishman, a slave to whiskey and a man I think very little of, as he is a tool." Late in the afternoon, Brady came into the Tunstall store. He was very disturbed and angry over the daily visits to the jail by Brewer and Tunstall. He accused Tunstall and Brewer of visiting with the criminals to assist them in making their escape.

Suddenly Tunstall threatened to kill Brady if he ever attempted to arrest him. He had his hand on a small pistol concealed in his jacket and aimed directly at Brady's heart. But the flare was over as soon as it started and Brady left the store without bloodshed. The next day a new jailer was found but Brady kept the keys. The discussions between Tunstall and Jesse Evans would have long range implications.[56]

In November, Brady's efforts to restore peace were shattered when the inmates of the jail successfully made their escape. However, all Lincoln knew was that Billy Bonney, alias Billy the Kid, Lucas Gallegos and several other criminals had arranged for the escape of their friends.

Francisco Trujillo and his brother Juan were hunting deer in the Pajarito Mountains when Billy the Kid and his companions from the Penasco River area passed on their way to Lincoln. Early the next day, Bonney, Evans, Baker and Gallegos returned to the Trujillo camp, took all their weapons and saddles, and headed toward the Rio Feliz. Devastated, the Trujillo brothers returned to their home in San Patricio.[57]

It is curious to note, after Tunstall made friends with the criminals and gave them whiskey (definitely against the law) that Evans and his gang escaped from jail just two days later. They immediately headed for Brewer's ranch, another friendly hide-out. Tunstall's meeting with Evans obviously resulted in an understanding. Evidently Tunstall was certain the boys could be used to further his schemes for Lincoln County. Furthermore since Tunstall's horses and mules were returned to him by Jesse Evans, he did not press charges or have the thieves arrested. Instead they became friends. And without a warrant Brady's hands were tied. He had no authority to go after the Evans gang.[58]

Early in December prior to his interrupted trip to St. Louis, Alexander McSween sold the east wing of his home to his sister-in-law Elizabeth Shield. The total price of the transaction included one dollar plus "consideration with love and affection." This hasty decision on the part of McSween to sell most of his home must have lifted some eyebrows. The deed conveyed five rooms to Shield with an internal wall separating the two households. After the transaction was completed, McSween put his business affairs in order and prepared for his extended trip to St. Louis.[59]

On December 7, 1877, Administrator Charles Fritz filed a petition asking the Probate Court to order Alexander McSween to deposit the proceeds from the insurance policy in the court fund. As early as August 1877, McSween filed an earlier petition demanding an account of the Fritz Estate that had not been completed. From all appearances, this petition was just another ploy by McSween to prevent Charles Fritz and Emilie Scholand from receiving the insurance money. McSween still had the money tied up in the Merchants' National Bank in St. Louis, the same bank used by John Henry Tunstall. McSween failed to comply with the court's request.

Approximately two weeks later, Emilie Scholand who had been living in Clifton, Apache County, Territory of Arizona returned to Dona Ana County, New Mexico to file a formal complaint of embezzlement against McSween. She was convinced that McSween had kept the money.[60]

Immediately, Warren Bristol, Judge of the Third Judicial District, authorized the issuance of a warrant for McSween's arrest. On the day the warrant was issued, McSween and his wife were headed toward Las Vegas, New Mexico to meet John Chisum. McSween's exit from Lincoln might be compared with cattle thieves who skulked in the woods until the posse had passed. After spending a few days in the town, the three continued to St. Louis on what was described as a business trip. The warrant for the arrest of McSween had been dispatched to Las Vegas and delivered to Adolph P. Barrier, Deputy Sheriff of San Miguel County. On December 27, 1877, both Chisum and McSween were arrested and placed in the county jail. Chisum's confinement had nothing to do with McSween's embezzlement charge. He had been detained on a civil charge and confined in jail for resisting an officer. Mrs. McSween was allowed to continue on the scheduled trip back east.[61]

Following a week of confinement in the Las Vegas jail, McSween was taken to Mesilla by Deputy Sheriff Barrier for arraignment before Judge Bristol on the charge of embezzlement. The next day formal charges were pronounced on McSween who was then released to Barrier. The court instructed the deputy to deliver McSween to Sheriff Brady in Lincoln. McSween was to either post bond or be kept in the county jail until the April term of court. On their way to Lincoln, Deputy Sheriff Barrier allowed McSween to escape because he believed that the lawyer could not receive a fair trial. Later, the court issued a warrant for the arrest of Barrier and charged him with contempt of court. It seems strange that a well-known deputy sheriff would jeopardize his office by allowing Mc-Sween to escape. Of course the escape could have been easily accomplished if there were some finanical inducements, or perhaps some other lucrative agreements.[62]

When Barrier released him, McSween headed for one of Chisum's cow camps located on the Pecos River. He intended to hide himself from the law until things quieted down in Lincoln. The apparent justification for this act is contained in a statement made by McSween before Special Investigator Frank Warner Angel in July 1878. McSween signed a statement that he believed his life would be in danger if he had been confined in the Lincoln County jail. [63]

Nevertheless, his flight to avoid prosectuion provided the citizenry with the possibility that McSween was not totally innocent of the charges. Therefore, the hasty act implied admission of guilt by McSween to embezzle the Fritz insurance money. Now it became obvious to the Administrators, Charles Fritz and Emilie Scholand, that the attorney did not intend to release the insurance money.

Therefore, on February 7, 1878, Charles Fritz and Emilie Scholand filed a lawsuit in the Third Judicial District Court against Alexander McSween to reclaim all the insurance money. They stated in the complaint that McSween promised to pay them in February but, under the circumstances, it was doubtful if the money would be recovered. Furthermore, it was their belief that the defendant, Alexander McSween, "intended to craftily and secretly deceive and defraud the plaintiffs." The court granted the $10,000 judgement against McSween together with interest and cost of the suit. [64]

Upon receipt of the judgment request, Judge Bristol issued a Writ of Attachment ordering Sheriff Brady to inventory all of McSween's property in town and wherever his property was to be found in the county to satisfy the suit. The sheriff then was to present the inventory at the April term of court to be held on the second Monday in April 1878. The date of the April term of court for Lincoln County had been previously established by the Territorial Assembly on January 6, 1874. Official records for the spring term of court (April 8, 1878), the second Monday in April, have not revealed changes contrary to the law. [65]

The judge then ordered Sheriff Brady to arrest and hold McSween in confinement until the first day of the April term of court. At that time, McSween would have to answer to the charges of embezzlement and the civil suit for $10,000. Brady had instructions from the judge to have McSween, the arrest warrant, the writ of attachment and the inventory in court on April 8, 1878. [66]

On February 8, Sheriff Brady and his deputy, George W. Peppin, enlisted a posse to assist them with the attachment and began inventorying the McSween property in Lincoln. The property consisted of the McSween house, adjacent land and buildings that included the Tunstall-McSween store and bank, and the contents of each building. The cattle and horses located in McSween's corral were also to be noted. [67]

It was determined that McSween not only had an interest in the store and bank but the cattle and horses grazing on the open range near the Rio Feliz. During the embezzlement hearing in Mesilla, the attorney admitted that he and Tunstall were partners in the same business enterprise. McSween testified that it was a temporary verbal agreement to be consumated by a written contract the following June.

However, Tunstall never agreed with McSween's interpretation of their alleged partnership. He did not intent to bind himself to any type of business contract unless it favored his schemes. It is quite obvious, though, that Tunstall must have made some sort of agreement similar to his land project. Tunstall used McSween to advise him on the business activities. The entrepreneur always found a way to keep McSween involved. McSween was right where he wanted him. [68]

While the sheriff continued with the attachment of the property, McSween spent his time trying to make bond on the embezzlement charge. Within a few days McSween returned to town with a surety bond of $35,000. The District Attorney, William L. Rynerson, rejected the bond because he was not convinced that the sureties were solvent. McSween was kept under surveillance and permitted to continue with his efforts to post bond. [69]

However, Tunstall was in the store to check on his part of the property. The fact that he was angry and extremely upset over the attachment proceedings is understandable. He had record books, contracts and other papers that most certainly would have revealed the partnership business activities in Lincoln county.

There were some rumors that Tunstall claimed ownership of the horses located in McSween's corral. Therefore, he requested, or forced, Sheriff Brady to exempt them from the inventory. After reviewing the inventory, there is no evidence that such an event ever took place. Brady always kept accurate records, indicative of his military training. Certainly he would have disclosed this transaction if only to keep track of the animals. But the writ of attachment did not provide for exemptions. However, the inventory revealed four saddle horses owned by McSween and valued at $200. [70]

Tunstall's favorite horses, stolen by the Evans gang in October, were placed on the Rio Feliz by the end of November 1877. He had been delighted that the horses had been returned by Jesse Evans. But the animals were in poor physical condition and needed to be left on the open range to recuperate. On several occasions he had to use a common saddle horse, which he found distasteful.

On February 12, 1878, Sheriff Brady sent this deputy, Jacob B. Mathews, who had with him George W. Hindman, John Hurley, Andrew L. Roberts and Manuel Segovia to attach all of the horses and cattle in the area near the upper Rio Feliz. McSween and Tunstall owned the personal property there under a joint business venture agreement.

When Mathews and his posse arrived at the Rio Feliz they were met by Robert Widenmann and 15 armed men who refused to allow the deputy to carry out the legal writ of attachment. Mathews quickly returned to Lincoln and reported the incident to Sheriff Brady.[71]

Meanwhile Tunstall had been informed of the attempt to attach the horses and cattle on the Rio Feliz. He and his recently acquired ranch hands, William Bonney, alias Billy the Kid, and Fred Waite, left Lincoln and headed for the ranch on the Feliz. Their purpose for leaving town, of course, was to round up the horses and cattle and remove them from the ranch. The horses grazing on the open range would become Tunstall's nemesis and ultimately cause his death. Surely if any of the animals had been exempt from the attachment then it is conceivable that the horses would not have been confiscated. But if the horses were not removed from the inventory, then Tunstall had every reason to believe they would be attached.[72]

More than likely, the latter condition formed the basis of Tunstall's decision to remove his horses as soon as possible. He loved his horses and intended to protect them in every way possible. Furthermore, it is interesting to note that while Tunstall and his cohorts were on their way to the Rio Feliz, they stopped by the Chisum South Spring Ranch requesting help, but were refused. The Chisum group must have sensed or anticipated the possibility of trouble ahead. Later, Bonney claimed that Chisum promised to help finance "the soldiers."[73]

When Tunstall arrived at the Feliz ranch, he decided to circumvent the law and probably take his horses to some remote area of Lincoln County. Because he knew a posse was on its way, Tunstall executed a plan immediately to save his horses. Tunstall always boasted how clever he was and how he developed schemes in such a way that no one would suspect his motives. This particular incident certainly required a scheme, and certainly Tunstall believed he could avoid the attachment by relocating his prized horses.

But back in Lincoln, Sheriff Brady immediately set his own plans in motion. Because of the circumstances involved with the attachment proceedings at the Feliz, Brady increased the posse to 24 men and again sent Mathews to carry out the attachment. The sheriff had to stay in town with his posse to guard the other attached property and prevent further violence. Brady also admonished the deputy sheriff "not by any means call on or allow to travel with your posse any person or persons who are known to be outlaws." As a former military officer, Sheriff Brady was well accustomed to issuing specific instructions in order to achieve intended results. Since J. B. Mathews was a recently deputized peace officer and since the conditions at the Rio Feliz were tenuous, Sheriff Brady's request showed great wisdom — a genuine effort on his part to keep the peace.[74]

On the morning of February 18, 1878, Tunstall, Billy the Kid, Brewer, Middleton, Billy Wilson and Robert Widenmann collected the horses and headed in the direction of Lincoln off the main traveled roads. Tunstall intended to hide the animals in some remote cow camp. Later that same morning Deputy Sheriff Mathews and his posse arrived at the Rio Feliz and cautiously approached the ranch. But this time they found no one there except a neighbor, Martin Mertz, and the cook, Godfrey Gauss. As the posse approached the ranch house, Gauss informed Mathews that Tunstall had left with the horses earlier that morning. Both Mertz and Gauss were then assigned as representatives in charge of the Tunstall-McSween property.[75]

The deputy sheriff now called his posse together to form a plan. Mathews decided to separate the posse, sending part of them after the thieves to recover the stolen animals. Mathews deputized William Morton as head of a sub-posse with instructions to arrest Tunstall and his devious ranch hands and attach the horses. Each member of the Morton posse had been carefully identified. Late in the afternoon of February 18, 1878, Deputy Sheriff Morton, together with 13 men including John Beckwith, George Hindman, J.W. Olinger and Manuel Segovia, left the ranch to arrest the criminals. Those posse members who stayed behind were scheduled to inventory the remaining property under the direction of Mathews.[76]

The Morton posse had traveled only a short distance from the ranch when the deputies realized that Tunstall had taken a circuitous route away from the main trails. According to reports, somewhere along the new route Jesse Evans, Frank Baker, Tom Hill and John Long joined the posse. Evans had loaned some horses to William Bonney and intended to recover them. He had no interest in the attachment proceedings. Furthermore, Tunstall and Evans were friends.[77]

Within a few hours, the posse finally located Tunstall who, with his ranch hands, had driven the horses into a small canyon. Perhaps Tunstall or someone else in the group had seen the posse and intended to make a stand against the deputies. The posse continued toward the scene to arrest the thieves. It was almost nightfall making it difficult for the posse. Moments later shots were fired. Tunstall was dead.

About 10 p.m., Widenmann and Bonney rushed into town with the news for McSween. Strangely the posse returned to the Rio Feliz sometime after midnight, and neither Tunstall's companions nor the posse arranged to have the body brought to Lincoln. The horses were not located. And why would anyone leave a body in that desolate area as prey for wild animals? "Rob" Widenmann was Tunstall's close associate and certainly he should have taken the responsibility. Tunstall's letters to his family reflected Widenmann's loyalty: "He [Widenmann] is a splendid fellow and takes as much care of me as if I were a woman." But not this time.[78]

Meanwhile since Bonney did nothing to help his boss, the legendary close association with Tunstall became questionable. Tunstall had never referred to Billy the Kid in any of his letters. But he did discuss Jesse Evans frequently and intimated their friendship. Still important is the fact that Richard Brewer and John Middleton, foreman and assistant respectively, did nothing to care for the body after Tunstall's death. Finally the story has it that McSween asked John Newcomb, who owned a ranch near the death scene, to bring the body to Lincoln.

Two days later, assisted by the medical missionary, Dr. Taylor F. Ealy, the Assistant Surgeon of Fort Stanton, Dr. David M. Appel, conducted a post mortem examination, the body was embalmed, and Tunstall was buried in a vacant lot directly behind the store. Interestingly, Dr. Ealy was new in town having only arrived the day before the examination. McSween had encouraged the missionary to come to Lincoln to establish a church and missionary school.

In July 1878, Dr. Appel made a sworn statement before the federal investigator, Judge Angel, regarding the autopsy performed on John H. Tunstall:

"That on or about the 21st day of February 1878, I made a post mortem examination of John H. Tunstall. I found that there were two wounds on the body, one in the shoulder passing through and fracturing the right clavicle near its centre, coming out immediately over the superior border of the right scapula passing through in its course the right sub clavicle artery. This wound would have caused his death within a few minutes and would have been likely to have thrown him from his horse. It would not have produced immediate insensibility. The other wound entered the head about one inch to the right of the median line almost on a line with the occipital protuberance of the left orbit. There was a fracture of the skull extending around the whole cirucumference from the enterence to the exit of the ball, and a transverse fracture across the middle portion of the base of the skull extending from the line of fracture on one side to that of the other. In my opinion the skull both on account of its being very thin and from evidence of venereal disease was likely to be extensively fractured from such a wound and this fracture in this case resulted entirely from said wound. A wound of this kind would cause instantaneous death passing as it did through the most vital portion of the brain. There were no marks of violence or bruises on the body except the above two wounds nor was the body or skull mutilated. The cap of the skull was not at all fractured. It is my opinion that both of the wounds could be made at one and the same time, and if made at the same time were made by different persons from different directions and were both likely made while Tunstall was on horseback inasmuch as the directions of the wounds were slightly upwards.

There being no powder marks on the body to indicate that the wounds were made at a short distance and the further fact that the edges of the wounds at exit were not very ragged, I am of the opinion that they were made by rifles. Powder marks would be shown on the body if the gun or pistol was fired within about six feet of the body." [79]

Several conflicting stories surrounded the death of Tunstall suggesting that the unfortunate incident had been authorized by Sheriff Brady. But during his investigation of the troubled county in July, the special investigator, Judge Angel, had collected sworn affidavits from various individuals who supplied different accounts of Tunstall's death.

Perhaps Morton's version may have some validity since he was the only one who admitted shooting at Tunstall. His statement was in the form of a letter mailed by Ash Upson from the Roswell Post Office to his cousin, H. H. Marshall of Richomond, Virginia.

Morton stated that he had been called to assist in serving a writ of attachment on the Tunstall-McSween ranch and other property near the Rio Feliz. Before he arrived at the scene, Tunstall and others had taken horses from the ranch which should have been attached. Mathews then appointed Morton as a deputy sheriff and after a posse had been selected, they went in pursuit of the criminals. Within a few hours, the posse overtook the thieves. During this time, Tunstall's cowboys scattered and left the area. While Morton attempted to serve the writ Tunstall fired at the posse. The deputies returned the gunfire killing Tunstall. [80]

Billy Wilson's account offered a different point of view. Wilson was a member of the Tunstall party that had taken several horses from the ranch at the Rio Feliz. About 15 or 20 miles from Lincoln, Tunstall and his men saw the posse coming toward them. The horses then were driven into a small canyon for protection. Wilson stated that Tunstall told his men to stay with the horses about 100 yards from the posse and be ready to give him help if it became necessary. He (Tunstall) would meet with the deputies and discuss the situation. Tunstall then rode toward the posse. Approximately 30 yards from the deputies, words were exchanged and subsequently Tunstall was shot and killed. Since it was getting too dark to see a target, Tunstall's men retreated deeply into the canyon where they concealed themselves from the posse.[81]

Because of the varying reports concerning the Tunstall incident, the Justice of the Peace, John B. Wilson, empanelled a coroner's jury to determine how the Englishman met his death. As an apparent eyewitness to the alleged murder, Widenmann could not testify that he saw Tunstall shot and could not name the men who shot him. Jesse Evans had been mentioned as a suspect in the case. But Evans stated that he had been more than 25 miles away from the scene on that day. At that time, no one seemed to know for certain who had shot Tunstall. Yet warrants would be issued later by Wilson's court to apprehend certain members of the legally deputized posse. But for now, Wilson would exceed his authority if he acted. Tunstall had died outside his jurisdiction.[82]

CHAPTER 5
NOTES

1. Lincoln County, **Assessment Records 1875.** Assessor's Office, Lincoln County Courthouse, Carrizozo. Map identifying Brady's homestead in author's collection. (See also homestead patent and improvements, NA, RVA, RG 15, CWLP, WO-555-976.)
2. Keleher, **Lincoln County,** p. 33.
3. Lincoln County, **District Court Records** (April 1876). NMSRCA. (See Biography of David Abraham, Public Library, Silver City, New Mexico.)
4. Lincoln County Records (November 1880). NMSRCA.
5. Westphall, **Thomas Benton Catron,** pp. 79-81.
6. Keleher, **Lincoln County,** p. 34.
7. **Ibid.,** p. 35.
8. Fulton, **Lincoln County War,** pp. 95-9.
9. Keleher, **Lincoln County,** p. 36.
10. **Ibid.,** pp. 37-9.
11. J. H. Tunstall To My Much Beloved Governor, (March 12, 1877); Fulton Papers, Box 14; Special Collections, Universtiy of Arizona Library, Tucson.
12. Lute Jackson to John Chisum, **Bill of Sale** [no date]. Lucien B. Jackson Papers, Oklahoma Historical Society, Oklahoma City.

13. Bennett Leroy Brady to Author (February 9, 1983).
14. **Congressional Record**, 44th Congress 1877, Section 11; **Desert Land Act**, Ch. 107, Sec. 2, p. 377.
15. J. H. Tunstall To My Much Beloved Governor, (March 23 1877); Fulton Papers, Box 14; Special Collections, University of Arizona Library, Tucson.
16. **Ibid.**
17. J. P. Tunstall To My Dear Boy, (March 28, 1877); Fulton Papers, Box 14; Special Collections, University of Arizona Library, Tucson.
18. First National Bank of Santa Fe, Archives 177; **Individual Ledger Book** #2, p. 615. Special Collections, Zimmerman Library, University of New Mexico, Albuquerque.
19. **Ibid.**, p. 616. **Transfer Ledger Book** #5, p. 112.
20. **Ibid.**, p. 699. **Blotter Book**, p. 147.
21. John To My Much Beloved Father, (April 21, 1877); Fulton Papers, Box 14; Special Collections, Universtiy of Arizona Library, Tucson.
22. J. H. Tunstall To My Much Beloved Father, (April 27, 1877); Fulton Papers, Box 14; Special Collections, University of Arizona Library, Tucson.
23. **Ibid.**
24. Bennett Leroy Brady to Author (February 9, 1983).
25. Lincoln County, **District Court Record 1875-1879**; case #242, p. 261. NMSRCA.
26. John To My Much Beloved Father, [no date]; Fulton Papers, Box 14; Special Collections, University of Arizona Library, Tucson.
27. Fulton, **Lincoln County War**, pp. 75-77. **Independent** August 18, 1877.
28. **Ibid.**, pp. 78-9. **Independent** August 25, 1877.
29. John To My Much Beloved Father, (June 8, 1877) Fulton Papers, Box 14; Special Collections, University of Arizona Library, Tucson. (See Mullin collection; **Freeman Ranch on the Penasco.** Nita Stewart Haley Memorial Library, Midland, Texas.)
30. Lincoln County, **Assessment Record 1877**. NMSRCA.
31. **Ibid.**
32. J.H. Tunstall To My Much Beloved Father, (April 27, 1877); Fulton Papers, Box 14; Special Collections, University of Arizona, Tucson.
33. Mullin Collection, Nita Stewart Haley Memorial Library, Midland, Texas.
34. First National Bank of Santa Fe, Archives 177; **Transfer Ledger Book** #5, p. 112. Susan E. Barber To Maurice G. Fulton, White Oaks (June 27, 1926). Fulton Papers, Box 1, Special Collections, University of Arizona, Tucson.
35. First National Bank of Santa Fe, Archives 177; **Individual Ledger Book** #2, p. 698. Special Collections, Zimmerman Library, University of New Mexico, Albuquerque.
36. Territorial Records, **Auditor's Disbursement Journal 1873-1880**. NMSRCA.
37. Territorial Records, **Treasurer's Ledger of Receipts 1870-1882**, p. 82. NMSRCA.
38. Territorial Records, **Executive Record Book 1878**, p. 334. NMSRCA.
39. Fulton, **Luncoln County War**, p. 105. (See Keleher, **Lincoln County**, p. 64; Nolan, **John Henry Tunstall**, pp. 261-62.)
40. Keleher, **Lincoln County**, p. 65. (See Fulton, **Lincoln County War**, p. 106.)

41. Bennett Leroy Brady To the Author (February 9, 1983.)
42. Lincoln County, **District Court Records 1875-1879.** Fall Term, pp. 228-262.
43. Lilly Klasner, ed. by Eve Ball, **My Girlhood Among the Outlaws,** (Tucson: University of Arizona Press, 1972), pp. 169-70. Bennett Leroy Brady, **Statement.** (See Fulton, **Lincoln County War,** p. 69.)
44. J. H. Tunstall To My Much Beloved Father, (August 19, 1877); Fulton Papers, Box 14; Special Collections, University of Arizona Library, Tucson.
45. **Ibid.**
46. J. H. Tunstall To My Much Beloved Father, (April 27, 1877); Fulton Papers, Box 14; Special Collections, University of Arizona Library, Tucson.
47. Bennett Leroy Brady, **Statement.** (Keown and Associates To the Author August 13, 1984.)
48. J. H. Tunstall To My Much Beloved Governor, (July 21, 1876); Fulton Papers, Box 14; Special Collections, University of Arizona Library, Tucson.
49. Lincoln County, **Assessment Records 1877-1881.** NMSRCA.
50. Lincoln County Records, **Commissioner's Record Book 1876-1879,** p. 26. Clerk's Office, Lincoln County Courthouse, Carrizozo.
51. Klasner, **Among the Outlaws,** p. 174. (See also Fulton, **Lincoln County War,** pp. 88-9.)
52. Fulton, **Lincoln County War,** p. 90.
53. Gus Gilda to Maurice G. Fulton, (August 9, 1927); Fulton Papers, Box 2, Special Collections, University of Arizona Library, Tucson.
    Gus Gilday, who was also called the "Young Texan," the "Texas Ranger," and "Buckskin," had arrived in Lincoln during the early stages of the conflict. In his letter to Fulton, Gilda states that he did not associate himself with either Murphy or McSween. Furthermore, the Seven Rivers Party was also not allied with the Murphy-Dolan Group. "They (Seven Rivers Party) were defending themselves against the common enemy; the Chisum-McSween **et als** known as the 'Gold Diggers' gang. We commonly spoke of them as 'The Modocs' a name given them by a man in the Seven Rivers Party who had been in the Modoc War." In the same letter he continues: "I have read **so** many false reports about that so-called week [war] that I hardly know the truth as I did then. It was simply the rich vs the poor and the natural hatred against the Catholics as Murphy, Dolan **et als** were, but in my opinion and from my view point at the time the Murphy side was in the right."
54. John H. Tunstall To My Much Beloved Parents, (November 29, 1877); Fulton Papers, Box 14; Special Collections, University of Arizona Library, Tucson.
55. **Ibid.**
56. **Ibid.**
57. WPA Files: **Francisco Trujillo Interview** by Edith Crawford; translation by A. L. White. (San Patricio, Lincoln County, New Mexico, May 10, 1937, p. 1-2). NMSRCA.
    Francisco Trujillo, brother of Juan Trujillo Justice of the Peace in San Patricio, arrived in Lincoln sometime during the fall of 1877. He partici-

pated in the capture of the Evans gang and, through the influence of his brother Juan, became associated with the Tunstall-McSween faction. Trujillo was 85 years old at the time of the interview in 1937. His statements only verify specific individuals and incidences in which he personally was involved.

58. John H. Tunstall To My Much Beloved Father, (January 9, 1878); Fulton Papers, Box 14; Special Collections, Univeristy of Arizona Library, Tucson.

59. Lincoln County Records, **Deed Book B**, pp. 33-5. Clerk's Office, Lincoln County Courthouse, Carrizozo.

60. Lincoln County, **District Court Records**, Civil Case #141. NMSRCA.

61. San Miguel County, **District Court Records**, Civil Case #724 and #912. **Court Record Book**, pp. 303 and 337. NMSRCA.

62. Keleher, **Lincoln County**, p. 63.

63. Angel Report, **McSween Affidavit.** Westphall Collection, NMSRCA.

64. Lincoln County, **District Court Records**, Civil Case #141; **Exhibit E, Complaint.** NMSRCA.

65. Lincoln County, **District Court Record Book 1875-1879**, p. 264. NMSRCA.

66. Lincoln County, **District Court Records**, Civil Case #141; **Writ of Attachment.** NMSRCA.

67. **Ibid.**

68. J. H. Tunstall To My Much Beloved Father (April 29, 1877); Fulton Papers, Box 14; Special Collections, University of Arizona Library, Tucson. Houston Chapman Report to Mr. J. P. Tunstall (February 10, 1987); Mullin Collection, Nita Stewart Haley Memorial Library, Midland, Texas.

69. Fulton, **Lincoln County War,** p.111.

70. Lincoln County, **District Court Records**, Civil Case #141; **Inventory of McSween's property in Lincoln.** NMSRCA.

71. Fulton, **Lincoln County War,** p. 112. (Keleher, **Lincoln County,** pp. 81-2.)

72. **Ibid.,** p. 114.

73. Nolan, **John Henry Tunstall,** pp. 270-71.

74. **Independent,** March 30, 1878.

75. Fulton, **Lincoln County War,** p. 115. (Jim R. Martin to the Author, August 3, 1982.)

76. Lincoln county, **District Court Records**, Civil Case #141; **Inventory of property on the Rio Feliz.** NMSRCA.

77. **Mesilla News,** July 6, 1878.

78. John H. Tunstall To My Dear Parents (January 30, 1878); Fulton Papers, Box 14; Special Collections, University of Arizona Library, Tucson.

79. Angel Report, **Affidavit by Dr. David M. Appel, July 1878.** Westphall Collection, NMSRCA.

Dr. Appel, Assistant Surgeon, Fort Stanton, was more than familiar with different forms of venereal diseases. The infectious diseases had almost reached epidemic proportions at many of the forts. Certainly he was capable of making an intelligent diagnosis when he performed the autopsy on John H. Tunstall.

80. Keleher, **Lincoln County,** pp. 99-100.
81. **New Mexico Historical Review,** University of New Mexico Press, Vol. 23, No. 2, 1948. "Notes and Documents," by Stephen A. Stone, pp. 146-155. (Jim R. Martin to the Author, August 3, 1982).
82. Grady E. McCright and James H. Powell, **Jessie Evans: Lincoln County Badman,** (College Station: Creative Publishing Company), p. 114.

Sheriff William Brady, Lincoln County, New Mexico (circa 1876).

View overlooking the town of Cavan (circa 1900).

The Cork Society of Friends Soup House during the Great Famine of 1847.

Roll call on the quarter deck of an emigrant ship leaving Ireland (circa 1847).

Fort Defiance, New Mexico in 1852.

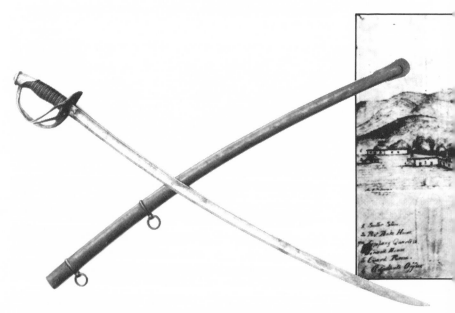

Sword that was presented to William Brady after his appointment as a lieutenant in the New Mexico Volunteers in 1861.

Troops from Fort Sumner, New Mexico. Bosque Redondo era; (circa 1864-68).

Drawing of Fort Stanton 1866.

Emil Fritz

Lawrence G. Murphy

Town of San Patricio, New Mexico shortly after statehood in 1912. The community was established by Irish soldiers who were mustered out of service in 1866. They include William Brady, James J. Dolan, Lawrence G. Murphy, John H. Riley and others. The building to the extreme left is believed to be the original Catholic church of St. Patrick erected by the Irish settlers in the 1870's.

John H. Riley

James J. Dolan

The Murphy, Riley and Dolan store in Lincoln, New Mexico just after Dolan had bought
out his partners. Porch added by Dolan in 1886.

89

Maria Bonifacia (Chaves) Brady, wife of William Brady (circa 1862).

Jacob B. (Billy) Matthews, his wife, Candelaria and children. Late 1870's.

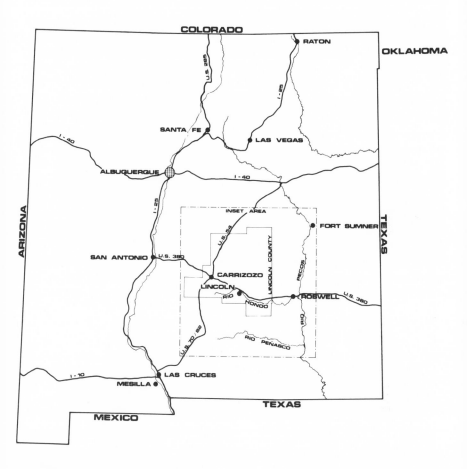

COLORADO

OKLAHOMA

RATON

U.S. 285

I - 25

SANTA FE

LAS VEGAS

I - 40

ALBUQUERQUE

I - 40

ARIZONA

TEXAS

I - 25

INSET AREA

FORT SUMNER

U.S. 54

SAN ANTONIO   U.S. 380

LINCOLN COUNTY

PECOS

CARRIZOZO

LINCOLN

RIO

HONDO

ROSWELL   U.S. 380

RIO

U.S. 70 82

RIO PENASCO

I - 10

LAS CRUCES

MESILLA

TEXAS

MEXICO

NORTH

0   50   100

MILES

Map: Lincoln County and vicinity.

91

John Henry Tunstall

Alexander A. McSween

Robert A. Widenmann

Frederick T. Waite

Susan (McSween) Barber

William Bonney alias Billy the Kid

Richard M. Brewer

William (Billy) Wilson alias Robert Levi Martin in his late thirties just before he settled down in Missouri.

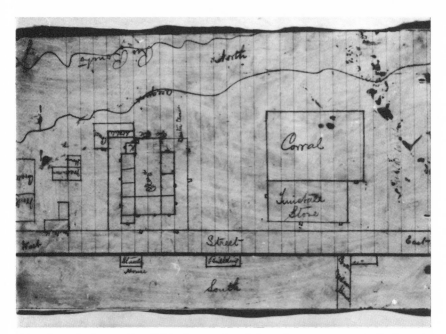

Map drawn by Deputy Sheriff John Long and used during his testimony in the Dudly trial regarding the burning of McSween's home; June 13, 1879.

Street scene in Lincoln, New Mexico (circa 1900).

West door of the Patron store in Lincoln. This is the one the Kid carved. It has since been removed.

Lincoln County courthouse after 1878.

Grave of William Brady in its present location on what used to be his property.

CHAPTER 6

ASSASSINATION

The day following Tunstall's death, Deputies Mathews and Morton reported to Sheriff Brady that the Englishman had been killed while resisting arrest when Morton attempted to serve the writ of attachment. The posse was a legally deputized body and the only one authorized to enforce the law in the county. Under the circumstances Sheriff Brady acted properly when he refused to issue warrants for the arrest of the posse. There was certainly no immediate proof that the posse had acted irresponsibly.[1]

In several letters to his family in England, Tunstall had mentioned that some day he would have to protect his property by force. "I think I can stand another fight if I am called upon." It is conceivable that Tunstall had indeed refused to turn over the horses to the posse. Also, he obviously did not intend to be arrested. He was confident "his boys" would assist him when it became necessary. But they did not. Tunstall's ring — so closely formed — had ultimately failed.[2]

After Tunstall's funeral, McSween called his forces together and planned a course of action against anyone involved in the death of Tunstall. This hasty action could be construed as a means to interrupt the proper channels to investigate the Tunstall incident. But more importantly, the meeting was held to determine who was loyal to McSween and to prevent his arrest by Sheriff Brady. McSween was still under indictment for embezzling the Fritz insurance money and regarded as a fugitive from justice; he had not been able to secure a bond. Some of his immediate supporters were William Bonney, Charles Bowdre, Richard Brewer, Frank McNab, John Middleton, Fred Waite and Francisco Trujillo. It was at this meeting that McSween offered $500 to anyone who would kill a member of the posse involved with the Tunstall slaying.[3]

Then McSween secured the services of the Justice of the Peace, J. B. Wilson, to deputize several of his supporters including the known outlaw, Billy the Kid. Wilson also deputized Tunstall's ranch foreman, Richard Brewer and Robert Widenmann who claimed to be an appointed

Deputy United States Marshall. These leaders then organized an illustrious group of so-called "loyal citizens" identifying themselves as the "Regulators." The local constable, Atanasio Martinez, had been authorized by the court to lead the posse and bring the suspects to justice. The arresting party included Constable Martinez and two regulators Bonney and Waite. After securing warrants, the men began a search for members of the legal deputized posse who were present when Tunstall had been shot. Since Brady was the county law inforcement officer, he refused to allow the arrest of any deputies and placed Martinez, Bonney and Waite in custody. But a short time later the three were released.[4]

The following day, McSween signed an affidavit before Judge Wilson charging Brady and his deputies with the unlawful appropriation of Tunstall's property. In an effort to keep peace and order, Brady and his deputies submitted to the arrest. The sheriff and his posse temporarily abandoned their efforts to attach McSween's property. All those named in the warrant were given a hearing before Judge Wilson. The judge confined Brady to his home under a $200 bond while Brady's deputies were released.[5]

During McSween's plot against the established legal authority, Sheriff Brady responded by sending a telegram to President Hayes requesting federal troops to assist him in maintaining peace and order. The telegram sent through Thomas B. Catron, Esq., U. S. Attorney, Santa Fe, New Mexico, and received by the President on March 4, 1878, contained the following message:

"Dear Sir

"A. A. McSween, wridaman [Widenmann] and others have collected a well armed mob of about fifty men and are still getting more to join them. They defy the law. They threaten the lives and property of our best citizens. The good and law abiding citizens although far in majority are not able to compete with them for want of arms. I cannot serve any legal documents or carry out the law if I am not assisted by the military. Please see his Excellency the Governor and ask him to obtain an order from Gen. Hatch to the Post Commander of Fort Stanton to protect me in the discharge of my official duties.

"I Am Very Respectfully Your

"Obediant Servant,

"Wm. Brady, Sheriff"[6]

Governor Axtell endorsed Brady's message to the President stating: "I know the sheriff and believe his dispatch to be true. One man an Englishman by the name of Tunsdell [Tunstall] has been killed. I start in the morning for the scene of action. It will take one four days to go there. I hope orders may be given to Gen. Hatch to send us such assistance as will enable me to keep the peace and protect life and property." On March 5, 1878, the Secretary of War, George W. McCrary, sent a message to Governor Axtell that the military can be ordered to support the civil territorial authority in monitoring order and enforcing legal processes.[7]

After receiving a telegram from the Secretary of War, Governor Axtell immediately left Santa Fe for Lincoln to determine the cause of unrest in the county. Since J. B. Wilson had been illegally appointed to serve as Justice of the Peace, the Governor quickly removed him from office and all processes by him were declared null and void. After making further inquiries into the troubled conditions in the county, the Governor, in a proclamation, officially reported that Judge Bristol, District Attorney Rynerson and Sheriff Brady were the only law in Lincoln. The Governor also removed Widenmann as a Deputy United States Marshall. The opposition was frantic to say the least, and charged that Governor Axtell was derelict in his duty when he refused to conduct a thorough investigation into the lawless conditions so prevalent in the county. The Cimarron **News and Press** claimed they received letters from prominent people in Lincoln reciting the indignation of the citizenry.[8]

On March 5 Brady sent a letter to the District Attorney W. L. Rynerson, concerning the near anarchy in Lincoln. Several weeks later, the Mesilla Valley **Independent** dated March 30, 1878, published Brady's letter. Brady reported to Rynerson that he and his deputies proceeded to the McSween store and levied the attachment in conformity with the law. While taking an inventory of McSween's property, Brady was "met at every step by insult and viterperation, [sic] and obstacles of every degree." He was also quite certain that while inventorying the property in the McSween home, "an accident alone saved me from assassination." Strangely, this statement was never explained.[9]

Brady continued his explanation of the attachment process at the Rio Feliz. When Deputy Sheriff Mathews arrived at the Tunstall place the first time he was met by an armed mob. Brady increased the posse and sent them to enforce the writ of attachment. When the posse reached the Rio Feliz they were informed that Tunstall and some of his cowboys had taken the horses from the ranch. A portion of the posse went after the men and in an exchange of gunfire, Tunstall was shot and killed. Brady also denied the existence of any known criminals attached to the posse.[10]

Brady also informed the district attorney that he had completed the inventory and placed men in charge of the property. However, Widenmann became involved with another party of reckless men including Bonney and Waite. They arrested the men Brady had placed in charge and took possession of the McSween property that had been attached. Brady pointed out the dangerous situation prevailing in Lincoln. "Anarchy is the only word which would truthfully describe the situation here for the past month, and the quiet and order now prevails, I fear very much that this condition of things will not last." [11]

The sheriff referred to the Justice of the Peace who had been used by the leaders of the mob. Although Brady did not mention his name, it is quite evident that the leader was Alexander A. McSween. Judge Wilson issued warrants of search and arrest indiscriminately against the posse and "all who in any manner countenanced against the mob." Brady had been arrested and released on a $200 bond. Brady said a terrible injustice had begun in Lincoln. "Private homes were entered under cover of this search warrant, and the inhabitants robbed and insulted by his so-called Constables. I await further instructions as to obtaining repossession of the property I attached." [12]

In a sworn affidavit dated April 18, 1878, George W. Peppin told his version of the episode at the Tunstall-McSween store. Peppin had been called on to assist in serving the writ of attachment. An angry mob arrested the posse and prevented them from continuing with the inventory. After the posse had been arrested, Peppin saw Sam Corbett, clerk in the store, hand the keys to McSween who allowed no one to enter the building. Two days later, Peppin stated that Sheriff Brady did not immediately retake possession of the McSween property because the sheriff was anxious to avoid bloodshed. His first concern was the peace and safety of everyone involved with the attachment proceedings. [13]

While Sheriff Brady had been prevented from finalizing the writ of attachment, he did have the inventory. Although the list was incomplete, it verified what appeared to be McSween's property valued at $7,379.50. However, this amount was not enough to satisfy the complaint. A final accounting would have to be made when hostilities subsided.

Shortly after Sheriff Brady and his posse were placed in close confinement, the recently formed "Regulators" began their quest for vengeance. To compensate for their failures and to earn the $500 reward offered by McSween, Brewer and several Regulators took it upon themselves to head for the Seven Rivers area south of Roswell. They were told that Baker and Morton were in the vicinity.

On March 6, 1878, The Regulators captured the suspects south of Chisum's ranch near the Penasco. During the return trip to Lincoln, the

Regulators murdered Baker and Morton because it was said the two men attempted to escape. Since he openly declared himself the protector of the prisoners and was anxious to have the men returned to Lincoln, William McCloskey was also killed. Furthermore, the Regulators suspected that he was a Dolan spy and considered him a threat to their organization. When they completed their assignment the Regulators then headed for McSween headquarters in San Patricio to find refuge at the home of Juan Trujillo. Brewer then left for Lincoln and reported the episode to McSween. [14]

The following day the Regulators at the Trujillo home hired a Mexican boy to go to Lincoln for provisions and to collect the reward money that McSween had promised. Meanwhile, McSween, who had been informed of the recent events, again decided to make a quick exit from Lincoln and head for the Chisum South Spring Ranch. [15]

With all of the anger, hatred and hostility that surrounded Lincoln, it would seem almost unreasonable for anyone to venture into the county. Yet a newcomer found his way into Lincoln: Montague R. Leverson of Leverson Ranch, Douglas County, Colorado. He had been listed as a practicing attorney in Golden. Leverson came to New Mexico to establish an English colony somewhere in the territory. Although Leverson had never been to Lincoln County until 1878, he viewed the community as the "garden of New Mexico and a suitable location for a colony from Old and New England." [16]

Upon his arrival, Leverson headed for the Pecos and the John Chisum Ranch to locate some land for his new colony. McSween, of course, was present and discussed the county situation with him. After his indoctrination by McSween and Chisum, Leverson returned to Lincoln and wrote two letters. One was to Carl Schurz, Secretary of the Interior; the other to President Hayes. [17]

In the one to Carl Schurz, Leverson introduced himself and requested the Secretary to personally hand the enclosed letter to President Hayes. Leverson's scorching letter to the President represented his opinion on the disturbed state of affairs in Lincoln. He stated that the county problems were caused by the corrupt United States officials. Leverson requested the removal of the District Judge, District Attorney and Governor Axtell charging they plotted and contrived to murder Tunstall. He said J. B. Wilson's appointment by the County Commissioners was proper and the governor's proclamation removing the Justice of the Peace was illegal. Leverson informed the President that he would present more serious charges before an impartial investigation committee. [18]

It was Leverson's opinion that the President should replace Axtell immediately and appoint a governor who was more responsive to the needs of the people. Probably Leverson was thinking of himself and would have accepted the governorship of New Mexico had it been offered him. Eventually Leverson's interference in local matters and his suggestions for change were not entirely shared by members of the community or Washington. The newspapers labeled him a "dead beat and tramp." So by 1879, Leverson left the territory and returned to Colorado.[19]

But Leverson was not the only newcomer to outwardly express anger. In a letter to his friend Reverend Sheldon Jackson, the Presbyterian Missionary, Dr. Taylor F. Ealy, illuminated his true feelings about the conditions in Lincoln. The letter dated March 19, 1878, was written while the Ealy family temporarily occupied the McSween home. The attorney, Alexander A. McSween, was in seclusion at the Chisum Ranch. Ealy wrote that "McSween refuses to go to jail. He is being persecuted partly because he is Presbyterian. He is now a refugee. I can see no dishonor in it. They are a dirty set of Irish cut throats, and you know what their religion is."[20]

During this time, Jas. J. Dolan & Co. was experiencing financial difficulties. The company had mortgaged the store, merchandise and cattle located on the Pecos River, as security for a loan to Thomas B. Catron of Santa Fe. The necessity for the loan was partly due to over extension on past due accounts. Although the Tunstall-McSween Mercantile Store opened for business in November 1877, it had offered competitive merchandise at lower prices with term payments. In three months, the competition was beginning to cut deeply into Dolan's business activities. Dolan was anxious for immediate cash from his patrons in order to pay back his loan to Catron. Because Dolan's mercantile business was in default, Edgar Walz, Catron's brother-in-law, was sent to Lincoln to manage the affairs of the firm. Meanwhile Catron retained Dolan who continued as the proprietor of the store. However, final transfer of the property to Catron would not be concluded until June 1878.[21]

At this time Alexander McSween was still in hiding near the Chisum Ranch. On Friday, March 29th, efforts were made to apprehend him by Sheriff Brady who had a warrant for his arrest. Under authorization from the War Department, Brady was accompanied by a detachment of soldiers from Fort Stanton commanded by Lt. G. W. Smith to help enforce the law. When they arrived at the ranch, the attorney was not there and no arrest was made. While in hiding McSween had always been well guarded preventing Brady from properly executing the warrant without causing some injury to men on either side which Brady was anxious to avoid.

During the conversation with Sue McSween, who had just returned from the east, Sheriff Brady was informed that McSween was planning to enter town on Monday April 1, 1878. Since Lt. Smith was under orders to keep the peace, both he and Brady guaranteed McSween's safety. The arresting officers then decided to return to Lincoln and wait the arrival of the McSween party.[22]

The Governor's Proclamation had devastating effects on McSween and his adherents. They were convinced that it had removed any possibility for redress until they could arrange to have their case heard in court. But the possibility of military protection offered some hope for a court appearance. The proclamation also provided that the military could be used by Sheriff Brady to monitor order and to enforce legal processes.

McSween was aware of his predicament. He knew about the outstanding warrant for his arrest charging him with embezzling the Fritz insurance money. As an attorney, McSween understood the consequences of his act. He also knew the warrants that were issued by the former Justice of the Peace, John B. Wilson, authorizing the arrest of the sheriff's posse and prohibiting them to continue with the attachment proceedings on his property were declared null and void by Governor Axtell. Furthermore, he had certain information that Sheriff Brady had the formal orders in his possession, and intended to enforce the law.

Therefore, decisive action would have to be taken by McSween to prevent interference by Sheriff Brady. Since he had not been convinced of military protection, McSween sent a message to his men to meet him at the South Spring headquarters as soon as possible. Because the Regulators were in camp near the confluence of the Hondo and the Pecos Rivers, the men were easily located. They were able to pass freely between their camp and the Chisum Ranch.[23]

On Saturday, March 30th, a meeting was held at the ranch to formulate plans for the protection of McSween when he returned to Lincoln. The Regulators called into action were Billy the Kid, Charles Bowdre, Henry Brown, Jose Chaves y Chaves, James French, Fernando Herrera, Candelario Hidalgo, Frank McNab, John Middleton, Jesus Sais, John Scroggins, Francisco Trujillo, Juan Trujillo, Fred Waite and Robert Widenmann. Richard Brewer, John Chisum, Alexander McSween, his wife Sue McSween, and Doc Scurlock were already at the ranch waiting for "their boys."[24]

While the men were having breakfast McSween told them he intended to return to Lincoln in the next few days. The obvious intent of the Governor's Proclamation required him to be there to protect his property, especially his home. There were certain valuable records kept in his home involving him with the business ventures of Tunstall including pertinent documents concerning the embezzlement charges. After breakfast, McSween told his men to go into the ranch store and get whatever supplies they needed. It was understood that McSween would pay the bill. Other supplies would be provided by Juan Trujillo. The Ellis store in Lincoln was still another supplier when the band was in the vicinity. [25]

McSween recognized his desperate situation. He must find a way to secure his property, and at the same time prevent Sheriff Brady from arresting him. His men would provide the added protection. As a practicing attorney, McSween was completely aware of the law requiring the spring term of the district court to convene on April 8, 1878. The court record had confirmed the date and proper notice had been completed.

When the men finished gathering their supplies from the ranch store they returned to the meeting room. The attorney then asked his men to meet him in Lincoln the following Monday (April 1, 1878) because "as soon as I arrive, Brady is going to arrest me and you should not let him get away with it." McSween was convinced that his life was in danger. Therefore he made an offer to his Regulators: "if you kill Brady you shall earn a reward." So fearful was McSween of an attempt on his life that he was willing to pay his men any fee to assassinate Sheriff Brady. No definite sum had been mentioned but probably it was the same amount of $500 originally offered to murder any one of the opposition. Of further importance to McSween was the recovery of the writ of attachment and especially the warrant for his arrest held by Sheriff Brady. Final judgement on the disposition of the legal documents would have to be decided by Alexander McSween. No doubt the considerations were discussed by the Regulators. [26]

When the meeting adjourned the Regulators began their journey toward Lincoln via the Capitan Mountains, camping that evening at the Agua Negra. This particular route offered protection and avoided suspicion of a large force coming into town from Chisum's South Spring Ranch. Since he had been a member of the posse that murdered Baker, Morton and McCloskey, Brewer decided to remain behind and attend to his own ranch located on the Ruidoso. [27]

Early Sunday morning, the Regulators discussed plans to determine who should wait for McSween in Lincoln on Monday and protect him from being arrested by Brady. The Anglos would go to Lincoln and the Mexicans to San Patricio and wait for further orders. If help was needed, they would be called. The reason for the separation was obvious. As the self-appointed leader, Bonney informed the men "that Brady was married to a Mexican and that it was a matter of policy, all Mexicans being sentimental about their own." Scurlock was also married to a Mexican woman and he decided to remain at San Patricio.[28]

After the arrangements were finalized, the group of assassins headed for Lincoln to complete their assignment.

Later that evening, the Regulators came into town and camped along the Rio Bonito north of the Tunstall-McSween store. The following morning Billy the Kid, Henry Brown, James French, John Middleton, Frank McNab and Fred Waite met in the store to furnish McSween with the guard he requested. Charles Bowdre, John Scroggins and Robert Widenmann were stationed outside near the store. Bonney and his men were told that the McSween party had not arrived from Chisum's ranch. They had spent Sunday night some 10 miles from Lincoln at Trujillo headquarters in San Patricio.[29]

This same morning Sheriff Brady was also making his plans to recover the McSween property and arrest the attorney. He knew McSween was to be in Lincoln on Monday morning and requested his deputies to meet him at the building east of town which served as a courthouse. Several writers have stated that Brady and his deputies were on their way to the courthouse to post notices about the session of court in Lincoln being postponed until the following Monday. However, there was no misunderstading about when the session was to begin and no reason for Sheriff Brady to put up a notice indicating a change. But Sheriff Brady had both the writ of attachment and the warrant for McSween's arrest, and he was determined to enforce the law.[30]

Just before Brady and his deputies left the courthouse located east of town, Francisco Analla (Anaya) sent his 12 year old son, Timoteo, to warn Brady that Billy the Kid and his gang were going to ambush them near the Tunstall-McSween store. The Brady farm had been one of the first places Bonney worked when he came to the valley and the family knew him well. So Brady did not expect Bonney to ambush him. The sheriff told Timoteo: "If Billy is going to shoot me at all, he will meet me in the street."[31]

About 10 o'clock on that Monday morning, April 1, 1878, Sheriff Brady, George Hindman, John Long, J. B. Mathews and George Peppin left the courthouse and headed west for the Tunstall store. Brady scattered his deputies allowing added protection. But at this point, the McSween assassins saw the sheriff and his deputies and stationed themselves behind a high adobe wall on the east side of the store that narrowed down to a wooden gate. From this position, they had a clear view of anyone approaching from the east.[32]

As the officers approached the store, a blaze of gunfire ripped the air.

Brady was killed instantly, his body pierced by countless bullets.

Hindman was critically wounded and died within minutes after the shooting. The three remaining deputies managed to escape.

Moments later Billy the Kid and Fred Waite searched Brady's pockets for the warrants. Deputy Sheriff Mathews, who had concealed himself in the Cisneros house (called El Chorro) opposite the Tunstall-McSween store, fired at one of the men, possibly Bonney, wounding him slightly in the left thigh.[33]

Bonney quickly picked up Sheriff Brady's new rifle and disappeared behind the adobe wall. Waite followed Bonney and the other assassins to their camp on the Rio Bonito. Several hours later, the murderers reached McSween's house and remained there until nightfall when they returned to their hideout in San Patricio.[34]

CHAPTER 6
NOTES

1. **Independent** March 30, 1878.
2. John H. Tunstall To My Dear Parents (January 9, 1878); Fulton Papers, Box 14; Special Collections, University of Arizona Library, Tucson.
3. WPA Files; **Trujillo Interview** (1937), p. 2. NMSRCA. (See Fulton, **Lincoln County War,** pp. 379-80; and letter H. J. Chapman to John P. Tunstall February 10, 1879; Fulton Papers, Box 14; Special Collections, University of Arizona Library, Tucson.)

   I believe there is sufficient evidence to prove that Alexander McSween planned the assassination of Sheriff William Brady. Furthermore, the statements made by McSween's "boys" who were present at the McSween home and the Chisum South Spring Ranch in March 1878, are convincing.

   According to Francisco Trujillo, McSween offered $500 to his loyal supporters who killed a member of the posse involved with Tunstall's death. This is further supported by the McSween statement at the Chisum South Spring Ranch. "If you kill Brady, you will earn your reward."

   In February 1879, Houston J. Chapman (Sue McSween's attorney) wrote a letter to John P. Tunstall in England. In the letter, Chapman stated: "I desire to call your attention to the circumstances of the men who fought for your son and done all in their power to avenge his murder. They were promised both by McSween and Widenmann that they should receive pay for hunting down the murderers of your son."

In January 1880, Billy the Kid met John Chisum at Fort Sumner and the Kid took the opportunity "to make demand for $500 in payment **for services to the Tunstall-McSween-Chisum party's interest.**" Of course, Chisum felt differently about the debt. He claimed that McSween and party had been paid when they used his South Spring Ranch as a hide-out in March 1878. Also, he had let them have whatever they needed from his store on credit. At that point in the discussion, Bonney replied: "If you won't pay me **that** $500 in money I'll steal from your cattle until I get it." After that meeting, Chisum cattle began disappearing from the ranch in larger quantities.

4. Fulton, **Lincoln County War,** p. 126.
5. **Ibid.,** p. 127.
6. Sheriff Wm. Brady through Thomas B. Catron, U. S. Attorney, to President Hayes; Microfilm, M-666, Frame 51, NA, RG 397.
7. **Ibid., Endorcement #3,** Frame 55.
8. Fulton, **Lincoln County War,** pp. 144-45.
9. Sheriff Wm. Brady to W. L. Rynerson, District Attorney, 3rd Judicial District. **Independent,** March 30, 1878. [Author has not been able to find a full account of this incident.]
10. **Ibid.**
11. **Ibid.**
12. **Ibid.**
13. Lincoln County; **District Court Records,** Civil Case #141; **Affidavit by George W. Peppin.** NMSRCA.
14. WPA Files; **Trujillo Interview** (1937), p. 3. NMSRCA.
15. **Ibid.**
16. Interior Department; NA, RG 48, pp. 391-96. (Letters and attachments located in the **Frank Warner Angel Report,** Westphall Collection, NMSRCA.)
17. **Ibid.**
18. **Ibid.**
19. **Ibid.**
20. Ealy to Jackson, (March 19, 1878); Fulton Papers, Box 14; Special Collections, University of Arizona Library, Tucson. See Norman J. Bender, ed., **Missionaries, Outlaws, and Indians: Taylor F. Ealy at Lincoln and Zuni 1878-1881,** (Albuquerque: University of New Mexico Press, 1984), pp. 27-8.
21. First National Bank of Santa Fe, Archives 177; **Individual Ledger Book #2,** pp. 33-5. Special Collections, Zimmerman Library, University of New Mexico, Albuquerque.
22. Fulton, **Lincoln County War,** pp. 170-71.
23. WPA Files; **Trujillo Interview** (1937), p. 4. NMSRCA.
24. **Ibid.**
25. **Ibid.**
26. **Ibid.**
27. **Ibid.,** p. 5.
28. **Ibid.**

29. Fulton, **Lincoln County War**, p. 158.
30. Lincoln County, **District Court Record 1875-1879**, p.264; spring term of court, April 8, 1878. NMSRCA. Bristol to Dudley, Exhibits C and D, April 6 and 8, 1878. NA, LR, **Office of the AG, Main Series, 1871-1880**; Microfilm Roll #397. (NMSL, LC, SW, 978. 9, A235u.)

    On April 6, 1878, Colonel N. A. M. Dudley, Commander of Fort Stanton, received a message from Warren Bristol, Judge, 3rd Judicial District, that he would be arriving on Sunday and in view of the disturbing conditions in Lincoln, requested permission to stay at the fort. On April 8, 1878, Bristol again requested a troop escort to Lincoln to open the regular term of court. (See also Lincoln County, **District Court Record**, Civil Case #141, **Copeland Affidavit**. NMSRCA.)

    On April 12, 1878, John N. Copeland, who was appointed Sheriff of Lincoln County, had received the original writ of attachment found on the body of Sheriff William Brady. However, the warrant for the arrest of McSween was not located. Bonney must have secured the arrest warrant but certainly did not have time to retrieve the writ of attachment due to the fact that he and Waite were fired upon by Mathews.
31. Interview Bennett Leroy Brady (August 8, 1984).

    Jose Montano was visiting in the Analla (Anaya) home when this incident took place. He gave the story to the Brady family after the sheriff was assassinated. At the time, the courthouse had been located east of town in the Wilson home. Brady came directly from his home, located about 3 or 4 miles from Lincoln, and met his deputies at the courthouse before entering the center of town.

    A misconception by writers stated Brady and deputies were walking east from the Dolan store and the officers were shot in the left side. Brady and Hindman were shot in the back while walking west from the courthouse (Wilson house) passing in front of the gate attached to the Tunstall-McSween store.
32. Frazier Hunt, **The Tragic Days of Billy the Kid**, (New York: Hasting House Publishers, 1956), p. 51-2.
33. James D. Shinkle, **Reminiscences of Roswell Pioneers**, (Roswell: Hall-Poorbough Press, Inc., 1966), p. 4.
34. WPA Files; **Trujillo Interview** (1937), p. 6. NMSRCA. See Dudley to AAAG Head-quarters, Santa Fe, New Mexico, May 4, 1878; Relating to the Disturbances in Lincoln County; NA, LR, Office of the AG, Main Series, 1871-1880; Micro-film Roll #397: (NMSL, LC, SW, 978.9, A235u.)

CHAPTER 7
CONCLUSION

The main street was quiet as most of the Lincoln residents had concealed themselves in their homes and business establishments during the assassination. Several hours later the bodies of Sheriff William Brady and Deputy George Hindman were removed from the murder scene and transferred to the courthouse. The local authorities and close friends then notified the Brady family of the tragedy and advised them not to leave their home until the unsettled conditions in town became stablized.[1]

Mrs. Brady and the children were escorted to Lincoln the next day. Many of their friends and loyal supporters were on hand to assist them with funeral arrangements. In the afternoon, Catholic services were held for the two slain officers. Following the service Brady and Hindman were laid to rest in Lincoln cemetery. Later, the family had the bodies exhumed and reburied on the sheriff's property east of town.[2]

This sudden and vicious attack on the peace officers of Lincoln clearly demonstrated the desperate and unstable conditions in the county. The cowardly murder of Sheriff Brady caused irreparable damage to his family and friends and left a void in the lives of those who loved him — his wife and children.

The day before, shortly after the assassination of Brady and Hindman, John Chisum, Alexander McSween and his wife, Sue McSween, quietly rode into the town of Lincoln. The bodies of the slain officers were still visible in the street as they rode by them. They made no inquiries as to their assassins, and offered no assistance in the investigation of the crime or pursuit of the murderers. Instead they met the criminals at McSween's house and aided their escape to San Patricio hiding out at the home of a former Justice of the Peace, Juan Trujillo. The day of the sheriff's funeral, Chisum and McSween left town and arrived at their San Patricio headquarters to eat dinner with the murderers and to discuss their next course of action.[3]

During the meeting, it seems reasonable to assume that Bonney and his gang of hired killers provided McSween with a detailed report of the assassination. Also, Bonney must have turned over to his leader and apparent benefactor the warrant for McSween's arrest. He was not successful in his attempt to retrieve the writ of attachment. It had been found intact on the body of Sheriff Brady.

Although there were different stories told concerning the events of that fateful day, April 1, 1878, most of the apparent eyewitnesses agreed on specific details immediately following the shooting. William Bonney was seen climbing over the wall. He did search the body of Sheriff Brady. And he did take Brady's new rifle that had been purchased by the sheriff only a few weeks before.[4]

But little attention has been given to the motives associated with McSween and his Regulators to murder Sheriff Brady. Members of Brady's family — his grandchildren and great-grandchildren — informed this author that Sheriff William Brady had made arrangements to travel to Santa Fe after the April term of court to consult with territorial and federal officials concerning the lawlessness in Lincoln. He had knowledge of the perpetrators who contrived, schemed and plotted to continue the exploitation of the community.[5]

We must remember that Brady had become a citizen of the United States and a legitimate property owner. He also knew about the federal regulations to own government land. The most important requirement was citizenship. In contrast, Tunstall had not taken the oath of allegiance to the United States, and there seemed to be no evidence that McSween had made a declaration to become a citizen. The sheriff recognized that the schemes of both speculators to hold land could not be accomplished in an ordinary way. Brady was certain the Tunstall machine had developed a plan to deprive the county. In his view, the plan had many features similar to the programs that generated the chaotic state of affairs in Ireland. Although Tunstall and McSween seemed to be perfect examples of dedicated citizens, they instituted personal campaigns against anyone who became wise to their intentions.[6]

After Tunstall's death, McSween promised $500 to William Bonney or any member of his gang to murder the sheriff. Bonney had been assigned the task to relieve Brady of both warrants and with the Regulators, provide McSween as much protection as necessary to prevent his arrest. Vengeance may have played some role in the assassination of Brady and Hindman. But no one in the murderous crowd knew John Henry Tunstall personally except possibly John Middleton and certainly Robert Widenmann. Tunstall's letters testify to this fact.

It seems the only ones who had revenge on their minds were Richard

Brewer, Alexander McSween, Robert Widenmann and probably John Chisum. They had to hire a derelict group of known killers to carry out their foul deed. Why would Billy Bonney abandon his own rule of behavior for self-preservation by "jumping" over a wall in the face of three rifles, unless the monetary inducement was sufficient for him to carry out his assignment? Later in one of Bonney's statements, he testified that he would soon become the owner of several acres of land. [7]

Following the assassination of Brady and Hindman, the two opposing sides involved in the Lincoln County troubles were clearly defined. Sentiments favoring either McSween or Murphy-Dolan were distinct and outwardly visible. Before a new sheriff had been selected, a Texan by the name of Andrew L. Roberts and Richard Brewer, Captain of the Regulators, were killed at Blazer's Mill. George Coe and John Middleton were both wounded. The Coe brothers left the country and, later, were involved in cattle rustling and the murder of Porter Stockton and his wife of Farmington, New Mexico. [8]

On April 10, 1878, the Board of County Commissioners met and appointed John S. Copeland as sheriff of Lincoln County. Two months later Governor Axtell removed Copeland from office because he had failed to file a bond as tax collector for the county. In every case, a sheriff is required by law to file a collector's bond within 30 days of his appointment. Two months had elapsed without Copeland attending to this responsibility. Copeland's response was that the tax list had not been prepared because of the disturbance in Lincoln County. Therefore, it was impossible for him to file a bond. However, previous sheriffs had filed their bonds within the appropriate time for $10,000 which is the amount set by law. More importantly though, the governor removed Copeland because the county commission again was not legally authorized to appoint a sheriff. The governor then appointed George Peppin to fill the vacancy until the November election. At that time, the citizens elected George Kimbrell as sheriff for a two year term. [9]

The grand jury for the April 1878 term of the District Court met to review certain matters concerning Lincoln County. One important case involved Alexander McSween, charged with embezzlement of $10,000 belonging to the estate of Emil Fritz. The foreman, Dr. Joseph H. Blazer, read a short statement prepared by the jury: "We were unable to find any evidence that would justify the accusation. We fully exonerate him of the charge, and regret that a spirit of persecution has been shown in this matter." Finally, McSween was successful in his attempt to avoid prosecution on the charge of embezzlement. The warrant for his arrest was missing. He had time to remove evidence involving him with the theft of the insurance money. The grand jury had no alternative but to release him.[10]

There was also a lawsuit that had been filed by the Administrators, Charles Fritz and Emilie Scholand, against McSween to collect on the $10,000 insurance policy. Because of attorney fees, surety bonds, court costs and various other legal entanglements, the heirs of Emil Fritz received very little of the inheritance that remained. During the entire episode, McSween never made an accounting of the Fritz Estate to the Probate Court. Finally Sue McSween failed to account for any balance on hand when she administered her husband's estate. The money just disappeared.[11]

On May 3, 1878, Brady's death was officially reported to the Montezuma Lodge in Santa Fe. Thomas B. Catron, Max Frost and David J. Miller were named on a committee to draft resolutions of regret.[12]

During the month of June, Judge Frank Warner Angel, as special agent for the Justice Department was conducting an investigation on specific matters concerning Lincoln County. He was instructed to concentrate on the death of John Henry Tunstall and the questionable management of the Indian Agency.[13]

Since the death of Tunstall, Montague Leverson, Alexander Mc-Sween and Robert Widenmann had been in contact with John's father, John P. Tunstall of London, England. The letters sent to the wealthy merchant requested that he exert his influence with the Prime Minister of England and insist upon an investigation into the death of his son. The language used in the letters had been designed to condemn the federal officials in New Mexico for their poor handling of the affairs in Lincoln County. In his legal opinion, McSween advised John P. Tunstall that he should be entitled to an indemnity. Armed with these reports John P. Tunstall was able to convince both the British and United States governments to examine the case. Young Tunstall was a British subject and this particular phase of the investigation had been conducted for political reasons to appease the English government.[14]

By July, political maneuvering became clear when the depositions had been completed by Judge Angel. With the assistance of Alexander McSween, Angel had been supplied with affidavits from "hand-picked" witnesses who presented a biased account of the troubled community. Many of the accounts were written by the capable Tunstall-McSween adherents, sanctioned by the attorney and signed by loyal supporters. The affidavit signed by William Bonney as an eyewitness to the Tunstall killing is quite obviously written by Widenmann.[15]

The affidavits were intended to exonerate McSween and his

followers. However, it has been clearly shown that McSween became deeply involved with land and mercantile schemes including Tunstall's financial affairs. Judge Angel's report was the last effort by the able attorney to clear his name. Three weeks later, he was dead. After several months had elapsed, his widow, Sue McSween, made the statement that she was left destitute as a result of her husband's death and the loss of her home. Yet, she moved to White Oaks and became known as the Cattle Queen of New Mexico. [16]

Judge Angel was also requested to look into the conduct of the management of the Mescalero Indian agency. Agent Frederick C. Godfroy seemed to be controlling the Indians well although some of the activities were questionable. He was later permitted to resign without being prosecuted. On the basis of what he had learned in Lincoln County, Angel concluded that the death of John Henry Tunstall was not brought about through corrupt United States Officials in the Territory of New Mexico. [17]

Continued political pressure forced the President of the United States to remove Governor Axtell from office appointing General Lew. Wallace as the new Territorial Governor of New Mexico. Shortly after Axtell's removal, Thomas B. Catron resigned as United States District Attorney. Despite the absence of any record in the Angel report that Catron was asked to resign, it is reasonable to assume some type of agreement existed indicating he should step down. Yet in August 1882, the President of the United States, Grover Cleveland, appointed Samuel B. Axtell as Chief Justice of the Supreme Court, Territory of New Mexico. When New Mexico became a state in 1912, the people elected Thomas B. Catron as the first United States senator from the new state. [18]

Another individual involved in the turbulent years of Lincoln county was Lawrence G. Murphy who died in Santa Fe on October 19, 1878. Twenty years later James J. Dolan passed away at his home in Lincoln, New Mexico. Most of the thieves and murderers who carried out the "dirty work" either left the territory or were killed before they had a chance to escape. After several attempts by the British government to collect on the death of John Henry Tunstall, the federal government concluded that there was no justification for the United States authorities to assume the collection of claims of its citizens. [19]

Through this entire episode, almost no effort was made to investigate the unprovoked assassination of Sheriff William Brady and Deputy George Hindman. There was no federal investigation ordered to institute a search into the matter, or to examine the facts to learn the truth behind this shameful act.

Shortly after Brady and Hindman were killed, William Bonney, Henry Brown and John Middleton were indicted for the murder. Two years later, the charges against Brown and Middleton were dropped because the District Attorney, Simon B. Newcomb, refused to prosecute the two killers. However, Bonney was still under indictment and later arrested. After killing two guards, Bonney escaped from jail and later was killed by Sheriff Pat Garrett on July 14, 1881.[20]

In August 1881, the Lincoln County Grand Jury met in special session and indicted Henry Brown, James French, John Middleton, John Scroggins and Fred Waite for the murder of Sheriff William Brady. In the indictment, the grand jury stated that the criminals with malice aforethought, unlawfully, feloniously, wilfully and from a premeditated design had murdered Brady. The sheriff was shot in the head, back and left side of his body resulting in instantaneous death.[21]

The reference to Brady being shot in the left side may very well be the answer for Widenmann's presence behind the adobe wall. Widenmann admitted being in the corral feeding a dog when the two officers were killed. But he was never indicted. From his position though he could have inflicted the wound to the left side of Brady's body. While in Mesilla, Widenmann received a letter from John Middleton who was living in Fort Sumner. Middleton informed Widenmann that he was a suspect in the murder of Sheriff Brady. Furthermore, "Old John [Chisum] has gone back on us and Ellis & Sons the same we don't ask no favors God dem them **Jesse Evans** is doing all he can for us say nothing about this whatever you do."[22]

The indictment of the five notorious outlaws was long overdue. Warrants were issued for the arrest of the criminals but the murderers were not to be found in the territory. According to the best available sources, there were nine men who actually participated in the assassination of Brady and Hindman. Within three years after the shooting, William Bonney alias Billy the Kid, Charles Bowdre and Frank McNab had been killed. Widenmann had left the territory for England to visit the Tunstall family. He did not stay long because John P. Tunstall asked him to leave the premises. And Widenmann never returned to New Mexico.

Mrs. Sue McSween survived the Lincoln County ordeal exceptionally well. On February 25, 1878, Alexander McSween had made a will designating John Chisum as the executor of his estate. In the event he could not fulfill the assignment, Sue McSween was named to succeed him. Since Chisum had left the territory, Mrs. McSween was then authorized by the court to be the recipient of her husband's estate.

Toward the end of 1884 news came to Lincoln that John Chisum had died in Eureka Springs, Arkansas.[23]

In November 1879, the court designated Sue McSween as administratrix for the estate of John Henry Tunstall. According to her reports, Tunstall did not own any property in Lincoln County. The estate was a financial disaster making it difficult to clear Tunstall's debts. After the estate had been settled, Mrs. McSween sold her property in Lincoln and moved to Three Rivers. Sometime later, she moved to White Oaks where she purchased a large cattle ranch. In June 1884, she married George Barber from whom she was divorced in 1891. Mrs. Barber managed the ranch for several years and in 1917, she sold the Tres Rios ranch to Albert B. Fall. Then Susan (McSween) Barber retired to her home in White Oaks where she died in 1931, at the age of eighty-six.[24]

When Sheriff William Brady was murdered on April 1, 1878, he had left behind a wife and eight children. His wife, Bonifacia Brady, was pregnant and gave birth to their last child in November 1878. The oldest child William Jr., was not quite 15 when the tragedy occurred. It became his responsibility to look after the household and manage the farm — not an easy task for such a young man. But as usual each member of the family made a contribution that eased the work load.[25]

On several occasions, Mrs. Brady requested aid and assistance from the Lincoln County Commission. Her husband had been an elected official killed in the line of duty and she felt the commission should accept part of the obligation and provide help to her family. The County Commission refused her request. However, the good friends and neighbors in the community were able to provide assistance until the family could manage for themselves.[26]

In 1880, tragedy once again invaded the Brady household. Lawrence Brady, while tending sheep in the Cloudcroft area near the Mescalero Reservation, was killed by Indians. On May 5, 1880, the Las Cruces **Thirty-Four** furnished an article about the sad event:

> "A gentleman writing from Lincoln under date of April 23rd says the Apaches are very bad and are stealing and killing at a terrible rate. They killed Jose G. Trujillo, Juan Chaves, and one of Mrs. Brady's boys and Bill Smith of the Penasco on the 18th. Also Sam Smith on the 21st, taking his team and destroying two loads of goods he was freighting for LaRue."[27]

For the next few years, operating the farm became expensive and debts were mounting with no relief in sight. Mrs. Brady's oldest children were married and had moved away from the farm. Since Mrs. Brady could not afford to hire anyone to operate the ranch, most of the work had to be done by the younger members of the family. In September 1881, the Probate Court of Lincoln County completed its findings on the estate of William Brady and granted all of the property to Bonifacia Brady and children.[28]

Hard times were quickly overtaking the Bradys leaving them almost destitute. James Dolan offered to buy the farm from Mrs. Brady and pay off her debts. The final agreement that had been arranged by the attorneys provided for the exchange of property mutually beneficial to both parties.[29]

On October 15, 1887, Mrs. Brady executed a warranty deed conveying the 320 acre farm to Dolan. Because of the children involved, a guardian deed was also required. Both deeds were certified and approved by the court. In the transaction, Dolan paid $1,600 in claims, debts and liens that had been assessed against the Brady family.[30]

Dolan then transferred 120 acres of cultivated land to Mrs. Brady that contained a ranch house and barn situated on the Rio Ruidoso in San Patricio, Lincoln County, New Mexico. An additional 80 acres of land adjacent to the Brady estate located on the Rio Bonito had been conveyed to the Brady children. The Brady family then moved into the new home at San Patricio and began farming the land. Bonifacia managed the farm for almost five years at which time she conveyed the 120 acres to her children. Because the property was legally divided before her death, a will was unnecessary.[31]

On July 28, 1892, Mrs. Brady filed a declaration for pension with the Bureau of Pensions, Department of the Interior as the widow of Major William Brady deceased. After a thorough investigation of the case, the Special Examiner, D. K. Fitzhugh, refused the pension because he was morally certain that Bonifacia Brady had remarried in 1883 to Joseph Carter. Maria Bonifacia Chaves de Brady died on May 23, 1898, and was buried on her property in San Patricio.[32]

There are many conditions, events and influences that help shape the life of every individual. The story of William Brady is an example of one human being who emerged from a relatively poor environment in Ireland, and then demonstrated through hard work, perseverance and tenacity that success can be achieved. During his formative years in Ireland, Brady and his family, along with many Irish citizens, had suffered terribly under the squalor of a depressed society that launched the Great Famine of 1845.

His desire to escape from conditions restricting his freedom and liberty where equal justice and opportunity were only designed for the aristocracy, convinced Brady to leave his homeland for United States. As immigrant, soldier, husband, father, citizen, legislator and sheriff, William Brady with each opportunity was able to adjust to the time and place and grasped each moment firmly.

He spent sixteen years in the cavalry and compiled an impressive military record. Those qualities that distinguish leadership were quickly recognized and Brady was soon appointed to lieutenant. He commanded troops and several forts and before his discharge, he had been commissioned a Brevet Major in the United States Army.

While in the military Brady married a native New Mexican, Maria Bonifacia Chaves, and after his discharge from service settled in Lincoln County. The predominant language of his adopted community was Spanish, so he acquired proficiency in that language. He was a devoted husband and father and encouraged by the new opportunities that had been afforded him. He became the first elected representative from Lincoln County to serve in the Territorial House of Representatives. Brady took an active part in community affairs recognizing the need for improved laws and dedicated officials. As sheriff, his most demanding considerations were law and order, protection for the citizens from land swindlers and continued peace in Lincoln County.

In reviewing the life and times of William Brady, it can be said that he served his adopted country with courage, dignity, honor and pride. He had faith in the land and its people and gave unselfishly of his time, his energy and finally his life in personal demonstration of that faith.

CHAPTER 7
NOTES

1. Interview Mabel Brady Neubauer (April 17, 1981).
2. **Ibid.**
3. **Weekly New Mexican,** August 10, 1878.
4. Interview Bennett Leroy Brady (August 8, 1984).
5. Bennett Leroy Brady, **Statement.**
6. Interview Mabel Brady Neubauer (April 17, 1981).
7. Keleher, **Lincoln County,** p. 296.
8. Territorial Records 1878-1881. Reel #99, frames 29-35. NMSRCA.
9. Lincoln County Records, **Commissioners Journal 1878,** p. 54. Clerk's Office, Lincoln County Courthouse, Carrizozo.

10. Fulton, **Lincoln County War,** p, 200.
11. **Ibid.,** pp. 197-99. Keleher, **Lincoln County,** p. 149.
12. **New Mexican,** May 18, 1878.
13. Keleher, **Lincoln County,** p. 246.
14. **Ibid.,** pp. 247-51.
15. Nolan, **John Henry Tunstall,** p.351.
16. Fulton, **Lincoln County War,** pp. 419-21. Keleher, **Lincoln County,** pp. 252-60. Angel Report, Westphall Collection, NMSRCA.
17. Westphall, **Thomas Benton Catron,** p. 127.
18. **Ibid.,** p. 134.
19. Nolan, **John Henry Tunstall,** p. 434.
20. Lincoln County Records, **Criminal Record Book, November 8, 1880,** Criminal Case #243. NMSRCA.
21. Lincoln County Records, **Grand Jury Indictment 1881,** Criminal Case #425. NMSRCA.
22. Nolan, **John Henry Tunstall,** pp. 386-87.
23. Keleher, **Lincoln County,** pp. 58-9.
24. Estate of John Henry Tunstall, **Probate Court Records 1881.** Clerk's Office, Lincoln County Courthouse, Carrizozo.
25. Interview Mabel Brady Neubauer, (April 17, 1981).
26. **Ibid.**
27. **Thirty-Four,** May 5, 1880. (Interview Mabel Brady Neubauer, April 17, 1981)
28. Estate of William Brady, **Probate Court Records 1881,** Case #52. Clerk's Office, Lincoln County Courthouse, Carrizozo.
29. Warranty Deed, October 15, 1887, **Book J.** pp. 188-89. Clerk's Office, Lincoln County Courthouse, Carrizozo.
30. Petition for Letters of Guardianship, File #53. Recorded in **Book A,** p. 93, November 7, 1887. Clerk's Office, Lincoln County Courthouse, Carrizozo.
31. Property Transfer from James J. Dolan to Bonifacia Brady et al. **Chancery Record Book,** September 12, 1888. (See Deed Book J, pp. 555-564) Clerk's Office, Lincoln County Courthouse, Carrizozo.
32. Department of the Interior, Bureau of Pensions, Washington, D.C. **Special Examiner's Report,** August 17, 1894. NA, RVA, RG 15, CWLP, WO-555-976.

BIBLIOGRAPHICAL SOURCES

Fort Craig, NM. Records of the U. S. Commands 1821-1920. LS and LR; GO and SO 1856-1865, vol. 1, NA, RG 393.

Fort Duncan, Texas. Muster Rolls and Orders of Company F, 1st United States Mounted Rifle Regiment August 1851 to March 1861. GO and SO; Post Returns and Morning Reports. NA, (Region 7, Fort Worth, Texas), M-617, R-335, RG 94.

Fort Seldon, NM. Returns from U. S. Military Posts 1800-1916. LS and LR; SO, Scouting Missions 1865-1866. M-617, R-1145, RG 94.

Office of the Quartermaster General, LS; Post Letter Book and Miscellaneous Documents 1866-1871. R-1, NA, RG 92.

Fort Stanton, NM. Returns from U. S. Military Posts 1800-1916. LS and LR; Morning Reports. M-617, R-1241, NA, RG 98..

Fort Sumner, NM. Judge Advocate General 1862-1869. Post Returns and Morning. NA, RG 98. Arrott Collection, Rogers Library, Highlands University, Las Vegas, New Mexico. Roll 10.

Fort Union, NM. Post Returns and Morning Reports 1851-1863. LS and LR; GO and SO. NA, RG 98. Arrott Collection, Rogers Library, Highlands University, Las Vegas, New Mexico. Rolls 1-3.

Lew. Wallace papers 1878-1881. Indiana Historical Society, Indiananpolis, Indiana.

Records of Enlistments U. S. Army 1849-1914. October 1850 to December 1854, vol. 49-50, p. 15. M-233, R-24, NA, RG 94.

Records Relating to the Dudley Inquiry. M-2097, R-1 and 2, NA, RG 153.

United States Army Commands. Department of New Mexico. LS and LR 1865-1870, Book 83. Arrott Collection, Rogers Library, Highlands University, Las Vegas, New Mexico. Rolls 8 and 9.

United States Census Records 1850-1880. NMSRCA. Fort Union 1860. Special Collections, Albuquerque Research Library, Albuquerque, New Mexico.

INTERVIEWS AND PRIVATE COLLECTIONS

Brady, Arcadio. Grandson of William Brady, Santa Fe, New Mexico. Provided pictures and materials.

_____, Bennett Leroy. Great grandson of William Brady, Roswell, New Mexico. Made available certain pictures of the family, the Brady Estate and pertinent documents and materials. Interviews February 9, 1983 and August 8, 1984.

Fulton Collection. University of Arizona, Tucson. Letters by John Henry Tunstall to his family in England. Various correspondence pertaining to Tunstall's movements in Canada and the United States. Particular emphasis on Lincoln, New Mexico concerning Tunstall's economic and political philosophy to exploit the county. Correspondence from some of the participants including letters from descendents of those who took part in the Lincoln County War.

Keown and Associates, El Paso, Texas. Information and Special Interpretation of Brady Reports August 13, 1984.

Lucian B. Jackson papers. Oklahoma Historical Society, Oklahoma City, Oklahoma. Bill of Sale to John Chisum and John H. Tunstall. Personal Interview with Lucian Boniparte Jackson, son of Lute Jackson, conducted by Jean

LaReau Miller, Archivist, Oklahoma Historical Society, March 1984.

Martin, Jim. Grandson of William H. (Billy) Wilson, Independence, Missouri. Provided correspondence that furnished summaries concerning Wilson's life in Arkansas, Arizona, Missouri, New Mexico and Texas including Mexico, August 3, 1982, and June 2, 1983. Contributed pictures of his grandfather and other pertinent data.

Mullin collection. Nita Stewart Haley Memorial Library, Midland, Texas. Interview with Jesus Ortega conducted by Robert Mullin, historian and author, Lincoln County, New Mexico, June 12, 1913. Letter from William A. Keleher, noted Lincoln County historian and author to Robert Mullin, November 1919. Documents emphasize the character of William Brady while in New Mexico. Other materials, notes, letter and documents pertaining to the turbulent conditions in Lincoln County, New Mexico.

Newbauer, Mabel (Brady). Great granddaughter of William Brady, Underwood, Minnesota. Taped interview with Mrs. Newbauer conducted by author April 17, 1981. Information provided insights on specific incidences in Lincoln, New Mexico as told by her grandfather, Robert Brady.

Tully, Bonnie (Brady). Granddaughter of William Brady, El Paso, Texas. Provided pictures and other documents.

Weisner, Herman. Historian, Organ, New Mexico. Provided copies of original documents concerning incidences and various individuals who participated in the Lincoln County troubles in the 1870s. Furnished other materials pertaining to the military 1866 to 1878.

Westphall Collection. "Report on the Death of John Henry Tunstall," by Special Investigator, Judge Frank Warner Angel. NMSRCA. Interviews and reports on the conditions in Lincoln County, New Mexico during the 1870s.

UNPUBLISHED MATERIALS

CHURCH RECORDS
Special Collections and Archives, San Felipe de Neri Church, Albuquerque, New Mexico, May 23, 1981.
Birth and baptismal records of Bonifacia Chaves, William Brady Jr. and Teodora Brady.

LIBRARY
Special Collections, Zimmerman Library, University of New Mexico, Albuquerque, New Mexico, December 30, 1981.
First National Bank of Santa Fe Records 1875-1878.
Personal bank records and ledgers of various individuals living in Lincoln County, New Mexico.

IRELAND
Diocese of Kilmore, Cathedral of SS. Patrick & Felim, Parish of Urney and

Annagelliffe, Cavan, Cavan County, Ireland. Patrick J. McManus, Administrative, V. G., November 21, 1979.

    Baptismal record of William Brady.

National Library, Dublin, Ireland. Alt MacLochlainn, Director, September 14, 1981.

    Directory of Cavan 1837.

    Microfilm register, parish of Urney and Annagelliffe.

    Voters register 1832; N. L. I. MSS. 9360.

    Photographic Archives.

Genealogical Office, Dublin Castle, Dublin, Ireland.

B. McKeen, Chief Herald, June 15, 1981.

    Heath Money Rolls; Griffith: Primary Land Valuations Cavan County.

    Genealogical record of the John Brady family of Cavan.

    T. 111, E. O. B.

Oifig An Ard-Chlaraithcora Custom House, Dublin, Ireland.

T. A. Meade, Ard-Chlaraitheoir Cunta, October 6, 1981.

    List of registers and records of families living in Ireland.

Public Records Office, Dublin, Ireland. P. Friel, Deputy Keeper, July 22, 1981.

    Census of Annagelliffe 1821.

    Testamentary Indexes 1877.

    Tithe Applotment Books, Urney and Annagelliffe, M.S. 2A-15-1.

    Book of Survey and Distribution, Cavan County.

    Pension Book M-3168, Cavan County.

    Kilmore Wills and Administration T-7432.

    Indexes to Kilmore and Prerogative Wills and Marriages; License bonds.

NATIONAL ARCHIVES

Bureau of Land Management. **Correspondence.** To the General Land Office, Santa Fe, New Mexico and others, 1872-1875. RG 49.

Certificate of Naturalization. vol. 2, July 1872. RG 49.

Homestead Patent Book 1875. Application #7, Certificate #4. RG 49.

Preemption Patent Book 1875. Certificate #10. RG 49.

Department of the Interior. Presidential Appointment 1860-1870. RG 48.

Department of New Mexico 1861-1870, LS and LR. RG 94.

Office of the Adjutant General 1780-1912. RG 94.

Office of the Quartermaster General 1794-1890. Bosque Redondo File 1865-1866. RG 98.

Office of the Veterans Administration. Military Files 1861-1866. CWLP, WO-555-976, RG 15.

Bureau of Pensions, Washington D.C. **Special Examiner's Report 1894.** CWLP, WO-555-976, RG 15.

NEW MEXICO STATE RECORDS CENTER AND ARCHIVES

District Court Records.

    Lincoln County 1869-1880.

    Santa Fe County 1863-1873.

Socorro County Book #3, 1865-1873.

Valencia County 1862.

Lincoln County Records.

Assessment Records 1870-1878.

Civil and Criminal Docket Books 1870-1878.

Commissioner's Record Book 1880.

Poll Books of Elections 1869-1876.

Various Deed Books 1869-1880.

McNitt Collection.

LS and LR from various military posts in New Mexico including command reports 1865-1866. (USAC, NA, RG 94 and 98.)

Office of the Adjutant General Territory of New Mexico.

Muster Rolls, Post Returns, Orders and Enlistment Records concerning various military posts in the department.

Schroeder Collection.

LR, SI, CIA, Appointments 1873. (USAC, NA, RG 48.) Description of the Mescalero Indian Reservation and Presidential Approval 1873. (NA, RG 48) Report of the Secretary of the Interior to the 42nd Congress, session 2, 1871. **Executive Document 1, Part 5, #1505**; 42nd Congress, session 3, 1872. **Executive Document 1, Part 5, #1560.** (NA, RG 396.)

Territorial Documents.

Auditor's Disbursement Journal 1873-1880.

Executive Records 1861-1882.

Legislative Records — **House Journal 1871-1874.**

Records of the Secretary of the Territory 1873-1876.

Treasurer's Ledger Receipts 1870-1882.

WPA Files.

Francisco Trujillo interview by Edith Crawford May 10, 1937.

LINCOLN COUNTY COURTHOUSE

Records of the Clerk's Office.

Brand Book B 1870-1879.

Chancery Records, property transfer 1888.

Commissioner's Record Book 1876-1879.

Deed Book E-Miscellaneous and Transfer Ledger Book C 1873-1876.

Patent Book F and Contract Book B 1871-1875.

Petition for Letters of Guardianship Book A 1887.

Probate Court Records concerning the estates of William Brady, Alexander McSween and John Henry Tunstall 1878-1881.

Warranty Deed Book H 1887.

Records of the Assessor's Office.

Abstract of Land Titles 1875-1887.

Survey Records and Maps 1878-1906.

THESES

Mechen, Lawrence L. **A History of the Mescalero Apache Reservation 1869-1881.** University of Arizona, 1968 (Masters).

PUBLISHED MATERIALS

GOVERNMENT DOCUMENTS

Annual report of the Commissioner of Indian Affairs 1865.
Washington. Government Printing Office, 1865.
Congressional Record, 27th Congress 1841, Session I.
"Preemption Rights Act." Washington. Government Printing Office, 1841.
Congressional Record, 37th Congress 1862, Session II.
"Homestead Act." Washington. Government Printing Office, 1862.
Congressional Record, 44th Congress 1877, Session II.
"Desert Land Act." Washington. Government Printing Office, 1877.
Office of the Adjutant General. Headquarters of the Army
New York. **Record Book.** Washington. Government Printing Office, 1858-1860. RG 94.
Prince, L. Bradford. **General Laws of New Mexico 1882.**
Albany. W. C. Little & Co., 1882.
Report of W. G. Ritch, Secretary of New Mexico, to the Commissioner of Education.
Washington. Government Printing Office, 1873. (See Territory of New Mexico, Legislative Records 1873. NMSRCA.)
The War of the Rebellion: The Offical Records of the Union and Confederate Armies.
Washington. Government Printing Office, 1891-1896.
IRELAND

Cunningham, Rev. T. P. D. C. L. "The Cavan Tenant-Right Meeting of 1850."
Breinfne. (Dublin), No. 12 (1969), 111-417.
Louis, Samuel. **Topographical Dictionary of Ireland.**
Dublin 2. National Library, 1837.
JOURNALS

Everett, Dianna, "The Public School Debate in New Mexico 1850-1891."
Arizona and the West, vol. 26, No. 2 (1984), University of Arizona Press, Tucson.
Stone, Stephen A., "Notes and Documents." **New Mexico Historical Review,**
vol. 23, No. 2 (1948), University of New Mexico Press, Albuquerque.
NEWSPAPERS

Las Cruces **Borderer,** 1871.
Las Cruces **Thirty-Four,** 1880.
Mesilla **Independent,** 1877-78.
New York **Daily Tribune,** 1846-47.
Santa Fe **Daily New Mexican,** 1868-1878.
Santa Fe **Weekly Gazette,** 1865.
Santa Fe **Weekly Post,** 1872.

OTHER PUBLICATIONS

Bender, Norman J., ed. **Missionaries, Outlaws, and Indians: Taylor F. Ealy at Lincoln and Zuni 1878-1881.** Albuquerque: University of New Mexico Press, 1984.

Bonney, Cecil. **Looking Over My Shoulder: Seventy-five Years in the Pecos Valley.** Roswell: Hall-Poorbough Press, Inc., 1971.

Emmett, Chris. **Fort Union and the Winning of the Southwest.** Norman: University of Oklahoma Press, 1965.

Fulton, Maurice G. Edited by Robert N. Mullin. **History of the Lincoln County War.** Tuscon: The University of Arizona Press, 1968.

Garrett, Pat. F. **The Authentic Life of Billy the Kid.** Albuquerque: Horn and Wallace Publishers, Inc., 1964.

Hace, Edward E. **Letters on Irish Emigration.** Boston: Phillips, Simpson and Co., 1852.

Hunt, Frazier. **The Tragic Days of Billy the Kid.** New York: Hastings House Publishers, 1956.

Keleher, William A. **Violence in Lincoln County.** Albuquerque: University of New Mexico Press, 1957. (first edition)

_____. **The Fabulous Frontier.** Albuquerque: University of New Mexico Press, 1962. (reprint)

Kelly, Lawrence. **Navajo Roundup.** Boulder: The Pruett Publishing Co., 1970.

Klasner, Lily, ed. by Eve Ball. **My Girlhood Among Outlaws.** Tucson: The University of Arizona Press, 1972.

Larson, Robert W. **New Mexico's Quest for Statehood, 1846-1912.** Albuquerque: University of New Mexico Press, 1968.

MacManus, Seumas. **The Story of the Irish Race.** Connecticut: The Devin-Adair Company, 1979. (revised)

McCright, Grady E. and Powell, James H. **Jessie Evans: Lincoln County Badman.** College Station: Creative Publishing Company, 1983.

McNitt, Frank. **Navajo Wars.** Albuquerque: University of New Mexico Press, 1972.

Moody, T. W. and Martin, F. X. eds. **The Course of Irish History.** 4 Bridge Street, Cork: The Mercier Press, 1976. (9th printing)

Nolan, Frederick W. **The Life and Death of John Henry Tunstall.** Albuquerque: University of New Mexico Press, 1965.

Norman, Edward. **History of Modern Ireland.** Maine: University of Maine Press, 1971.

Shinkle, James D. **Robert Casey and the Ranch on the Rio Hondo.** Roswell: Hall-Poorbough Press, Inc., 1970.

Utley, Robert M. **Frontiersmen in Blue: The United States Army and the Indians 1848-1865.** New York: The McMillan Company, 1967.

Westphall, Victor. **Thomas Benton Catron and his Era.** Tucson: The University of Arizona Press, 1973.

_____. **The Public Domain in New Mexico 1854-1891.** Albuquerque: University of New Mexico Press, 1965.

Woodham-Smith, Cecil. **The Great Hunger.** New York: Harper and Row, 1962.

INDEX

125

Scholand, Emilie (Fritz): 57-59,
    70-72, 112
Scholand, William: 57
Schurz, Carl: 101
Scroggins, John: 103, 105, 114
Scurlock, J.G. ("Doc"): 103, 105
Segovia, Manuel: 73, 75
Sena, Jose D.: 23
Seria, Joseph D.: 40-41
Shield, Elizabeth: 70
Sibley, H.H.: 23
Smith, Bill: 115
Smith, G.W.: 102-103
Smith, Sam: 115
Spiegelberg, Levi: 58
Spiegelberg, Willi: 36
Stockton, Porter: 111
Storms, Joseph: 51
Sullivan, A.P.: 37-38

Trujillo, Francisco: 70, 97, 103
Trujillo, Jose G.: 115
Trujillo, Juan: 70, 101, 103-104, 109
Trujillo, Serafino: 50
Tunstall, John Henry: 53-55, 59-78,
    97-99, 101, 104, 110, 112-113, 115
Tunstall, John Partridge: 53-54, 60,
    112, 114
Tunstall-McSween Mercantile Store:
    49, 61, 72, 99-100, 102, 105-106
Turner, John Hubert: 53
Twaddell, Harvey: 24

Upson, Ash: 77

Valdavios, Marcilino: 34

Waite, Fred: 74, 97-98, 100, 103,
    105-106, 114
Wallace, Lew: 53, 113
Walsh, Edward: 25, 27
Walz, Edgar: 102
West, James: 34
Wetter, Henry: 38-39

Widenmann, Robert W.: 54, 59,
    74-76, 78, 97, 99-100, 103, 105,
    110-112, 114
Wilson, Billy: 75, 77
Wilson, John B.: 41, 51, 53, 68, 78,
    97-101, 103
Wilson, William, d. 1875: 50
Wolf, Emil: 36